ARCHIVAL ARRANGEMENT AND DESCRIPTION

Edited with an Introduction by
CHRISTOPHER J. PROM & THOMAS J. FRUSCIANO

CHICAGO

Society of American Archivists
www.archivists.org

© 2013 by the Society of American Archivists.

All rights reserved. No part of this publication may be reproduced, stored in a retrieval system, or transmitted in any form or by any means without prior permission from the publisher.

Graphic design by Matt Dufek, dufekdesign@yahoo.com.

Library of Congress Cataloging-in-Publication Data

Archival arrangement and description /
edited with an introduction by Christopher J. Prom & Thomas J. Frusciano.
     pages cm. -- (Trends in archives practice.)
  Includes bibliographical references.
  ISBN-13: 978-1-931666-45-9 (print)
  ISBN-10: 1-931666-45-8 (print)
  ISBN-13: 978-1-931666-46-6 (eBook)
  ISBN-10: 1-931666-46-6 (eBook)
  ISBN-10: 1-931666-50-4 (pdf)
 1. Cataloging of archival materials. 2. Archives--Processing. 3. Cataloging of archival materials--Standards. 4. Cataloging of electronic information resources. 5. Cataloging of manuscripts. 6. Information storage and retrieval systems--Archival materials. I. Prom, Christopher J. II. Frusciano, Thomas J., 1950- III. Society of American Archivists.
  Z695.2A73 2013
  025.3'414--dc23
                        2013001202

Preface to
Trends in Archives Practice

Trends in Archives Practice marks an exciting new publishing initiative for the Society of American Archivists (SAA). For nearly forty years, SAA has provided the archival community with foundational manuals that have both established and reflected professional standards and best practices. Generations of graduate students and practitioners have used these authoritative texts to learn their craft and to develop policies and procedures for their institutions. These new modules continue that venerable tradition but also enhance our program in significant ways. For some time now, the SAA Publications Board has been investigating approaches to better serve our diverse audiences. Archival knowledge and literature has expanded exponentially in recent years. A complex and confusing array of acronyms, projects, and standards confronts all archivists. Most critically, the field is in the midst of rapid change, fueled by both theoretical breakthroughs and technological shifts. Clearly, our time-tested method for revising our foundational literature once every decade or so no longer is sufficient. The profession needs better and timelier access to basic information.

On a frigid February day in 2010, several Publications Board members gathered in New Brunswick, New Jersey, to grapple with this issue. Deborah Wythe, Joan Krizack, Thomas Frusciano, Teresa Brinati, and I considered a broad range of possibilities and ultimately concluded that a modular approach might best serve the needs of the profession. Thanks to a generous contribution from the SAA

Foundation, and with the support of the SAA Council, we convened a joint working group to flesh out the concept. Chaired by Helen Tibbo, it included Paul Conway, Thomas Frusciano, Gregory Hunter, Nicole Milano, Donna McCrea, Christopher Prom, Michael Shallcross, Nancy Beaumont, Teresa Brinati, and me. The idea for Trends in Archives Practice resulted directly from this collaboration. This new model sets a high standard for future endeavors and enhances our basic literature in several ways.

First, the three modules that constitute *Archival Arrangement and Description* complement Kathleen Roe's superb *Arranging and Describing Archives and Manuscripts* (Chicago: Society of American Archivists, 2005), which still serves as the standard introductory treatment of the topic. Roe noted in her introduction that "within a short time of its publication, readers of this manual will need to refer to contemporary archival literature for the most current status of practice" (xv). The *Archival Arrangement and Description* modules fulfill this prescient prediction by clearly and coherently synthesizing recent literature and addressing newer technological issues that have assumed center stage in the last decade. Readers who combine these modules with the Roe volume will have access to the foundational principles, theoretical bases, and current best practices that they need in order to approach arrangement and description with confidence and authority.

Second, the modules reflect a significant shift in SAA's approach to fundamental archival literature. Recognizing an industry-wide swing toward hybrid publication models, Trends in Archives Practice will be available in print and electronic formats. Planned future modules will expand on other volumes in the Archival Fundamentals Series II, wherein top-level professionals will be engaged to produce brief authoritative treatments that fill significant gaps in archival literature. The goal of this modular approach is to lead to a more user-centered publications program. Readers will be invited to mix, match, and combine modules that best satisfy their needs and interests. The *Archival Arrangement and Description* modules cohere nicely as a unified volume, but each authorial contribution also stands alone as a comprehensive examination of one discrete topic.

Finally, the modular approach stands as a monument both to continuity and to change. Over the years the SAA publications program has developed a well-deserved reputation for generating high-quality manuscripts that have made enduring contributions to the profession. Its distinguished authors and contributors have represented the most influential intellectual voices in the North American archival community. Trends in Archives Practice stands squarely in that tradition. It proudly gives voice to a new and innovative generation of archival leaders who are enhancing and enriching professional discourse. Further, it underscores SAA's commitment to provide students, practitioners, and archives professionals in general with the best in current practice and thought. But it does so in a nimble and easily updatable format appropriate for a fast-moving and rapidly changing record-keeping world. This new approach to archival fundamentals acknowledges the fact that our publications are living documents, necessarily fluid and constantly evolving. It seeks to balance our readers' need for up-to-date information with the careful deliberative review that they have come to expect from SAA products.

Archival Arrangement and Description has been edited by Christopher J. Prom and Thomas J. Frusciano. They are to be commended for their extraordinary effort in bringing these modules to fruition swiftly and efficiently without sacrificing our commitment to quality. Module authors Sibyl Schaefer, Janet M. Bunde, J. Gordon Daines III, and Daniel A. Santamaria proved a pleasure to work with in every way. Their contributions establish a high bar for future modules. Teresa Brinati and Anne Hartman at the Society of American Archivists have demonstrated tremendous flexibility and innovative thinking in developing a new model that will inform future publishing endeavors. We sincerely hope that you will enjoy and benefit from these collective efforts.

PETER J. WOSH
SAA Publications Editor
January 2013

Table *of* Contents

INTRODUCTION • 1
CHRISTOPHER J. PROM AND THOMAS J. FRUSCIANO

MODULE 1
STANDARDS FOR ARCHIVAL DESCRIPTION • 9
SIBYL SCHAEFER AND JANET M. BUNDE

MODULE 2
PROCESSING DIGITAL RECORDS AND MANUSCRIPTS • 87
J. GORDON DAINES III

MODULE 3
DESIGNING DESCRIPTIVE AND ACCESS SYSTEMS • 145
DANIEL A. SANTAMARIA

Introduction

CHRISTOPHER J. PROM AND THOMAS J. FRUSCIANO

Arrangement and description are the most fundamental of archival tasks and the most foundational. These activities are most fundamental in the sense that, without them, archival materials would remain lifeless, inaccessible, unknown, and unused; they are most foundational in the sense that they are typically the first tasks given to aspiring archivists, gifts that often bear fruit in a passion to make accessible the traces of human activity that we call archives and manuscripts.

However, the process by which we make these materials available—arrangement and description—can seem mysterious. If the ancient Greek philosopher Heraclitus had been a processing archivist, he might have written: "You cannot process the same collection twice, for other collections are ever flowing on to you." Or perhaps: "Arrangement and description are never the same."

All archivists confront change—change in the types and formats of documents we process, change in the context under which those documents were created, change in the topics and subject matter they document. But behind this change sit principles that inform all of our efforts to process materials and to make them accessible.

Development of Core Principles

Since 1977, the Society of American Archivists (SAA) has played a leading role in facilitating the means by which those core principles have been developed, communicated, revised, and extended. Not only has this entailed the development of standards to facilitate archival description (a difficult, consensual process, given what David B. Gracy II once called the kaleidoscope of descriptive practices used by archivists), it has involved the testing and refining of techniques to deal with new types of materials or to make materials accessible using new technologies.

The fruits of SAA's efforts have been most succinctly represented in manuals introducing the basic theories, methods, and practices that archivists use to arrange and describe materials acquired for their continuing value. These works are David B. Gracy II's *Archives and Manuscripts: Arrangement and Description* (1977), Fredric M. Miller's *Arranging and Describing Archives and Manuscripts* (1990), and Kathleen D. Roe's *Arranging and Describing Archives and Manuscripts* (2005), which were respectively part of the SAA Basic Manual Series, Archival Fundamentals Series, and Archival Fundamentals Series II.

As each author noted, his or her manual reflected theories and methods that were generally accepted at the time of publication. In this sense, each book distilled the knowledge generated during many conference presentations, professional publications, and informal discussions, resulting in a concise handbook that itself informed and shaped future archival practice.

Today, Kathleen Roe's manual remains essential reading for anyone hoping to learn about the fundamental concepts and techniques that facilitate effective arrangement and description; her volume also serves as a concise reference resource for practicing archivists. But as Roe herself noted at the time her manual was published, the specific standards, techniques, and practices that are used to arrange and describe archives must undergo a continual process of testing, refinement, and evolution, reflecting the evolution of society and the forms of documentation that result from human activity.

The Goal of These Modules

Since 2005, the theory and practice of arrangement and description have risen to meet the challenges posed by our mandate to document society in the digital era. Three areas of evolution are particularly noteworthy:

- the necessity to understand and use a range of descriptive standards to facilitate intellectual control and to improve access;

- the development of techniques to process "born-digital" or electronic records; and
- the methods used to make descriptive information about archives, and archival materials themselves, accessible via the Internet.

The goal of the modules is to draw together recent work in these areas. By so doing, these modules collectively aim to support learning and professional growth among students and archivists. The modules summarize recent literature and provide core knowledge regarding descriptive standards, tools, and services that support archival work to process records and to make them accessible. In this sense, the modules complement Roe's manual by building on its sturdy framework.

Each of the modules, in its own way, provides a more detailed description of standards, practices, and technologies, as they have evolved since 2005 and as they support the core archival functions described by Roe. By better understanding these developments, archivists will be well placed to put Roe's recommendations into immediate practice, as well as to build additional knowledge and skills by delving more deeply into recent archival literature regarding arrangement and description.

The Variety of Audiences Served

The purpose of publishing these modules is not to replace any manual on arrangement or description, but to provide relevant details that will allow archivists to become fully conversant with the basic standards, tools, and services that are necessary to accomplish archival work in the digital age. As such, the modules will be of use not only to students or archivists in training, but to *all* members of the profession who need an overview and summary of relevant work in these areas if they are to arrange and describe archives in a way that makes them optimally accessible, given a repository's goals, resources, and constraints.

While the modules that constitute *Archival Arrangement and Description* address the changing nature of archival content and descriptive practice, they also fulfill a need to disseminate a new core literature to a transformed archival profession. With the tremendous growth in graduate archival education programs over the past two decades, archival educators and their students are seeking information that captures and presents the most current thinking regarding archival theory and practice.

In assembling this core literature, archival educators structure their courses around readily available online resources rather than assigning introductory publications, and their students are accustomed to accessing course material on the Web. Archival educators mix and match from the rich and growing periodical literature, seek more theoretically sophisticated resources, and are interested in affordable, single-volume professional overviews. The modules offered in this volume meet that demand by offering the latest developments in the area of arrangement and description of archival records and manuscript collections in the digital age.

The archives profession also includes a growing number of practitioners with limited experience working with historical records. Core knowledge and foundational literature on the basic archival function of arrangement and description remains vital for these working archivists, and *Archival Arrangement and Description* makes that literature readily available. These modules are also essential reading for instructors and participants of the many popular and successful training programs and workshops offered through national and regional archival organizations; federal, state, and local government employees; tribal archivists; and religious archivists who seek sound literature that provides core archival knowledge.

Finally, these modules are also directed toward audiences outside the immediate archival profession. Digital technology has fostered a greater visibility for archival and manuscript collections in local libraries. Special collections have assumed more significance within academic libraries as colleges and universities have sought to highlight the materials that make their institution unique. In an era of full-text databases and shared resources, special collections have emerged as the distinguishing feature of academic libraries.

Public historians have incorporated archival materials into Web exhibits and created digital archives projects. Archives have partnered especially with social studies educators to tie their resources more closely to state and national standards and to create document-based curriculum for the K–12 community. Each year more than half a million students—encouraged by thousands of teachers nationwide—choose historical topics related to the National History Day contest theme and conduct extensive primary and secondary research through libraries, archives, museums, oral history interviews, and historic sites. It is essential that the most current theory and practice in arrangement and description be readily available to this generation of librarians, public historians, and educators who regularly incorporate archival materials into their daily work.

About the Modules on Arrangement and Description

In Module 1, *Standards for Archival Description*, Sibyl Schaefer and Janet M. Bunde provide a concise and passionate introduction to the world of descriptive standards. As the authors point out, the proper use of descriptive standards will help a repository ensure that its collections are described in a way that facilitates better access to the materials. The module provides a supreme and unique service in untangling the history of standards development and in providing an overview of most, if not all, of the descriptive standards that an archives might wish to use. The module discusses the standards in a logical order, helping anyone confused by the various acronyms to clearly understand the purposes and potential uses of each standard.

This module is particularly useful because it does not draw only on archival descriptive standards. It also references companion standards, developed outside of the archival community, that support archival work. By gaining a greater appreciation and basic understanding of each standard, any archivist will be much better positioned to decide whether it is appropriate for local use, to contribute to cross-repository initiatives, and to share descriptive records and digital archives in a user-friendly way.

In Module 2, *Processing Digital Records and Manuscripts*, J. Gordon Daines III applies concepts developed for the arrangement and description to electronic records or "born-digital" collections. While this is an area of emergent and evolving best practice, the module builds on familiar terminology and models to show how any repository can take practical steps to process born-digital materials and to make them accessible to users. By adapting the sample workflow provided in the module and by using some of the tools that are discussed (or other tools, as they emerge), a processing archivist can ensure that digital records are kept in a trusted way, ensuring their authenticity.

The piece is notable for showing how standards and tools developed outside of the archival community can be adopted to facilitate the processing of born-digital records. While the specific tools and services mentioned may not meet every repository's needs, and while additional tools and services are becoming available at a rapid rate, the information that Daines conveys will help any archivist become conversant with the fundamental concepts and techniques that will allow additional learning in this critical area, skills that must be mastered if we wish to exercise proper control over born-digital materials.

Sometimes archivists are given well-intentioned advice: "Why don't you just put everything online?" Leaving aside thorny intellectual property issues to hosting archival content (perhaps a topic for a future module), the mere question of how to choose and implement tools can seem perplexing. Module 3, *Designing Descriptive and Access Systems*, written by Daniel A. Santamaria, lists, describes, and provides implementation advice regarding the wide range of tools and software that support specific needs in arranging, describing, and providing access to analog and digital archival materials.

The virtue in Santamaria's module lies in the holistic way that it treats description and access. It describes and evaluates specific tools that can be used to complete specific archival tasks, making recommendations that will be suitable for a variety of archives. The options that Santamaria provides—basic, more advanced, and most advanced—demonstrate the wide latitude that can be used in implementing archival descriptive and access processes to meet local needs and capabilities.

Each module defines the core concepts that serve as foundational knowledge for the area discussed. In addition, the authors provide relevant examples of tools and services that support the work of arranging and describing archives and manuscripts. Ongoing and current developments, such as the emergence of new standards, are treated in a systematic way. The modules also include useful reference information and appendices, such as lists of further readings and comparisons of tools. Of particular interest are the case studies which provide practical examples of the concepts discussed in the main body of each module.

Some common themes emerge:
1. Good descriptive practices facilitate good end-user access.
2. Archivists must use professional judgment in assessing how to implement the standards, methods, tools, and services that support arrangement, description, and access.
3. While standards, tools, and services will continue to evolve, a good understanding of basic descriptive theory and practice, as well as a realistic assessment of repository capabilities, will allow archivists to select and use the technologies that are most suitable to repository goals.

Conclusion

Archival arrangement and description transform the record of people's daily activities into a living research resource that people can find, use, interpret, and repurpose. The standards, methods, and technologies described in these modules facilitate discovery and use in the digital age. Information about them should be part of every archivist's core knowledge, even as we realize that no one person or volume can ever write the final word on best archival practices. For that reason, we hope you learn much from these first modules—and that you watch for the release of additional modules in SAA's Trends in Archives Practice Series.

Christopher J. Prom is assistant university archivist and associate professor of library administration at the University of Illinois, Urbana-Champaign. Thomas J. Frusciano is university archivist at Rutgers University.

MODULE 1
STANDARDS FOR ARCHIVAL DESCRIPTION

SIBYL SCHAEFER & JANET M. BUNDE

Table *of* Contents

Introduction • 12

The Importance of Standards • 12
    What Are Standards? • 12
    Why Use Standards? • 15
    Standards and Archival Description • 16

Archival Descriptive Standards • 19
    Data Structure Standards • 20
        Machine-Readable Cataloging (MARC) Records • 21
        Encoded Archival Description (EAD) • 24
        Encoded Archival Context—Corporate Bodies, Persons, and Families (EAC-CPF) • 30
    Data Content Standards • 35
        Anglo-American Cataloging Rules (AACR) • 35
        Archives, Personal Papers, and Manuscripts (APPM) • 36
        General International Standard Archival Description (ISAD[G]) • 37
        Describing Archives: A Content Standard (DACS) • 38
        International Standard Archival Authority Record for Corporate Bodies, Persons, and Families (ISAAR[CPF]) • 41
        International Standard for Describing Functions (ICA-ISDF) • 42
        International Standard for Describing Institutions with Archival Holdings (ICA-ISDIAH) • 43
    Data Value Standards • 44
        Library of Congress Name Authority File (LCNAF) • 44
        Union List of Artists' Names (ULAN) • 45
        Library of Congress Subject Headings (LCSH) • 46
        Art and Architecture Thesaurus (AAT) • 47
    Metadata and Companion Standards • 48
        Descriptive Metadata • 49
        Structural Metadata • 51
        Administrative Metadata • 52
        The Semantic Web and Linked Data • 52

Archival Standards in Action • 54
    EAD Consortia • 54
    The Social Networks and Archival Context Project (SNAC) • 55
    Archival Data Management Software • 56
    Standards Revisions • 57

Archival Description for Your Repository:
Choosing the Right Standards • 58
    Institutional Factors • 59
        Descriptive Practice • 59
        Descriptive Resources • 60
        User Needs • 61
    Nature of the Materials • 61
    Community Context • 62

Conclusion • 63

Appendices
    Appendix A: Case Studies
        Summary of the UCSD DAMS System • 66
            by Bradley Westbrook
        What We Learned at ECU by Experimenting with EAC • 67
            by Mark Custer
    Appendix B: Further Reading • 69
    Appendix C: Acronyms Relating to Archival Description • 74

ABOUT THE AUTHORS

Sibyl Schaefer is the head of digital programs for the Rockefeller Archive Center, where she manages all digital services provided by the department, from digitization to curation. Schaefer previously served as the metadata librarian for the University of Vermont's Center for Digital Initiatives and also as the user services liaison on the Archivists' Toolkit project out of New York University. She has been recognized as an Emerging Leader by the American Library Association (ALA) and is currently a member of the Society of American Archivists' Technical Subcommittee for the revision of DACS and a co-chair of the ALA Digital Preservation Interest Group.

Janet M. Bunde currently serves as the assistant university archivist and archivist of the John Brademas Congressional Papers at New York University (NYU). She received her MA in history with a certificate in archival administration from NYU in 2007. Her areas of professional interest and research include both advocacy and incorporating archival materials into educational instruction. Bunde also serves as the director of Outreach and Advocacy for the Archivists Round Table of Metropolitan New York.

Introduction

This module provides an overview of standards currently used in archival description. No one standard is fully explored, and not all standards are covered. Only established, widely adopted standards and those newly developed or recently embraced by the archival community are included. The appendices of the module include a list of resources for readers who want additional information on standards that may be relevant to their repositories' specific descriptive needs.

The module is divided into four sections. The first discusses the general importance of standards and their specific applicability in archives, noting that archival descriptive standards can be grouped into three types—data structure, data content, and data value. The second section discusses fourteen national and international archival descriptive standards in depth, providing descriptions and examples where needed. It also covers four metadata and companion standards that were developed outside the archival community but have archival applications. The third section focuses on the future of archival standards and includes a brief description of archival management software, collaborative projects that leverage description across repositories, and current plans to revise existing standards. Section four offers guidelines that will help archivists and repository staff to determine which standards best meet local needs. Please note that after a standard is first introduced, it is referred to by its acronym. Appendix A provides case studies, Appendix B a list of additional readings, and Appendix C definitions for all acronyms.

The Importance of Standards

What Are Standards?

Standards are a necessary part of society and everyday life. Standards allow you to use the same electrical outlet for different appliances and the same credit card at different retailers. Standards are developed and defined through consensus and for several purposes. First and foremost, they enable interoperability between systems. They define common sets of vocabulary for different concepts, easing data exchange among information systems. Standards also enable shared practices within a profession, lowering the barrier for collaborative projects; if two institutions use the same vocabulary and practices, a foundation of mutual understanding is already present.

Standards, as defined by the Society of American Archivists (SAA) Standards Committee, are "an industry agreement that establishes qualities or practices that make possible sharing of information, development of common vocabularies and practices, and more effective interaction among archivists, librarians, records managers, information managers, preservation administrators, historians, and other allied professionals."[1] Applied in an archival setting, standards are used to support archival functions, such as delineating preservation systems (like the Open Archival Information System model, or OAIS), building archival facilities, and describing archival material. This document will discuss the last function, including standards used to describe digital archival material.

Standards greatly influence user expectations. If you buy a toaster in the United States, you expect to be able to plug that toaster into a typical U.S. outlet. Likewise, when you visit a Web page, you expect the navigation to be located at the top or down the left-hand side of the screen. Although both electrical outlets and Web navigation can be developed using standards, there is a significant difference between the two. The standard that applies to electrical outlets was defined by the National Electrical Manufacturers Association (NEMA) and is considered a de jure standard, or a standard formally declared by a major standard-setting body (see Figure 1). However, not all de jure standards may be widely used or supported, while other practices may be widely used without formal sanction. The placement of Web navigation can be considered a de facto standard—a practice that becomes standard through widespread adoption and use. Many de facto standards become de jure standards, although that is not always the case. Website designers may choose to place navigation in different areas, but going against the conventional placement may affect the usability of that website because such an action violates user expectations. User expectations greatly influence discoverability; the more standardized the format within which information is captured, the more a user can learn about searching for that information.

---

[1] Society of American Archivists, "Standards Development and Review," last revised January 2012, accessed August 20, 2012, http://www.archivists.org/governance/handbook/standards_com2.asp.

> **Figure 1. Who Sets Standards?**
>
> A standards-setting organization is an agency whose function is to develop and maintain standards. In addition to industry-specific standards-setting organizations, such as the National Electrical Manufacturers Association, there are several major standards-setting bodies. Internationally, the largest and most established of such entities is the International Organization for Standardization (ISO). ISO is made up of a network of national standards-setting bodies representing 164 different countries.[2] The American National Standards Institute (ANSI) serves as a member of ISO and works in conjunction with the National Institute of Standards and Technology (NIST), the U.S. government standards-setting body, to create U.S.-specific standards. The Internet Engineering Task Force (IETF) and the World Wide Web Consortium (W3C) are standards-setting bodies of a different sort; they define the technologies that sustain the Internet and the Web, such as TCP/IP, SMTP, MIME, HTTP, HTML, XML, and CSS.[3]
>
> Like many professions, the archival profession has its own standards-setting organizations, the largest being the International Council on Archives (ICA). The ICA's Committee on Descriptive Standards and the Society of American Archivists (SAA) have developed and maintained many of the standards related to archival description. Within SAA the Standards Committee is charged with "initiating and facilitating the development of standards; providing review and comment on standards that are relevant to archival theory and practice; educating the archives community about the value and role of standards; and partnering with related information management professional organizations on standards of mutual concern and interest."
>
> For additional information about standard-setting bodies, see the following websites:
> - http://www.iso.org
> - http://www.w3.org/standards
> - http://www.icacds.org.uk/
> - http://www.archivists.org/saagroups/standards/

Users are not the only consumers of information—computer systems are as well. Just as users learn that title information will exist in a title field, computers can be programmed to process or parse

---

[2] International Organization for Standardization, "ISO Members," accessed August 20, 2012, http://www.iso.org/iso/home/about/iso_members.htm.

[3] Worldwide Web Consortium, "Standards," 2012, accessed August 20, 2012, http://www.w3.org/standards.

that field systematically. In a networked world, standards support interchange and interoperability of data so that computers can index and display that data in a predictable fashion.

The process of setting and maintaining standards is initiated by professional organizations, but the implementation—and ultimate success—of these standards is up to individual archivists. As Daniel Pitti, a leader in developing standards for the archival profession, writes, "The success of any standard depends upon broad community participation in its development, followed by widespread recognition of the standard's utility."[4]

Why Use Standards?

Standards enable efficient production, description, and use of objects and information. Standards save time in manufacturing or designing items. To return to the example described above, toasters can be mass-produced and widely sold because they incorporate standardized components, are built to fit standardized sockets, and operate using standard voltage. In the same way, a website designer does not need to rearrange basic navigation features for each project she undertakes; she can rely on her knowledge of where users have come to expect to find these features.

Standards also make it easier for people to use objects and search for information. While most electronic devices, including toasters, come with operating instructions, they tend to work in a similar way and to offer similar features. A toaster that worked in a radically different way would require users to learn something new before obtaining their toast. The nonstandard device would slow down or confuse potential users, and it could even deter them from using it. Likewise, users of information can search for and interpret information more quickly and easily when it is described or organized in standard ways. Once they have learned the "language" of standards, they can exploit this knowledge to discover information and to better understand search results, with less effort being dedicated to learning the system. When information is not described or organized using a standard, users may face barriers to finding and interpreting information, or they may simply not find the information that they are seeking, even though it is included within the system they are using.

---

4   Daniel Pitti, "Encoded Archival Description: The Development of an Encoding Standard for Archival Finding Aids," *American Archivist* 60 (Summer 1997): 279.

Finally, standards lay the groundwork for not-yet-realized systems of producing, grouping, or discovering information. For example, a website designer might monitor developments in searching or indexing websites and decide to incorporate certain portions of code into her websites, in order to make the pages more visible in certain searches. Additionally, data that is described in a standardized fashion can be more easily ingested into and manipulated by computerized searches. An awareness of and investment in adhering to standards, then, gives a website or information a greater chance of being discovered and used in the future.

Standards and Archival Description

It is important to adhere to standards when describing archival materials because their use allows archives to record consistent, findable metadata about collections and records held within repositories. SAA's *Glossary of Archival and Records Terminology* defines archival description as "the process of analyzing, organizing, and recording details about the formal elements of a record or collection of records . . . to facilitate the work's identification, management, and understanding."[5] Four concepts raised by this definition are important.

1. Archival description is an iterative process. Archival description typically evolves over time, rather than being developed fully at once and never revised. As Richard Pearce-Moses notes in the definition cited above, archival description must be changed when additional materials, or accretions, are added to a collection. But description can begin before an archivist ever encounters archival materials. Some information about these materials is generated and maintained by creators and collectors before physical custody is transferred to archivists.[6] Archivists also capture descriptive information during the accessioning process as they bring materials into the repository.
2. Description is an active process, one that requires archivists to decide how and at what level to describe archival materials.

---

5   Richard Pearce-Moses, "archival description," in *A Glossary of Archival and Records Terminology* (Chicago: Society of American Archivists, 2005), accessed October 30, 2012, http://www2.archivists.org/glossary/terms/a/archival-description.
6   International Council on Archives, *ISAD(G): General International Standard Archival Description,* 2nd ed. Adopted by the Committee on Descriptive Standards, Stockholm, Sweden, September 19–22, 1999, accessed August 20, 2012, http://www.icacds.org.uk/eng/ISAD(G).pdf. See specifically sections I.2 and I.3.

How we describe the collections in our care influences the ability of people to discover, access, use, and interpret them. Archivists do not passively record what they see in individual items within a collection; they assess and explain the relationships of various records and records creators to each other. In other words, they record information about both the *content* of the records and about the *context* of their creation and use. Description does not necessarily end with the publication of a finding aid. Additional information about the nature or context of the materials or their creators may influence subsequent or revised descriptions of a collection or even an individual item.
3. Description can apply to an entire collection, a single item, or to many intermediate descriptive levels, such as record groups and series. In this way, archival description differs from bibliographic, or library-based, description, which most frequently occurs at the item level—the level of the book, monograph, journal article, or other publication being described. This flexibility allows archivists to employ a multitude of descriptive approaches (from item-level cataloging to broader collection-level description).
4. Description not only facilitates the dissemination of knowledge by making materials available to others, it also provides significant benefits to the archivist. Consistent archival description allows archivists to manage their collections more easily. Description also allows archivists to share information with both colleagues and users. Users, in turn, can make better use of materials that are well described, and good description facilitates new uses through data mining, textual analysis, and other advanced research methodologies.

Robust archival description covers four major areas: context, content, structure, and function.

Context. As mentioned above, archival description differs from bibliographic description because of its focus on the context surrounding the creation of the collection. Archivists add information about the person, family, or organization that created the records or manuscripts. This information typically includes the history of the organization whose materials are represented in a collection or a biography of an individual collector or creator, as well as other data elements. This contextual information sheds light on the materials in a collection by providing information about the circumstances under which the materials were created and used.

Content. Archivists provide inventories or descriptions of the materials in a collection so that researchers can see what types of documents exist in a particular collection and what information those materials contain. Sometimes, archivists also provide information about what kind of documents cannot be found in a collection.

Structure. As mentioned above, archival description differs from bibliographic description because it communicates the hierarchical organization of the materials and the relationships between archival materials, rather than flatly describing only the entire collection or single items within the collection. Within a collection, archival materials fall into natural groupings. The records of an organization, for example, may be categorized as administrative records, financial records, or legal records, among other categories. The group of financial records may also contain natural groupings such as records related to income, records related to expenses, and records related to taxes. Likewise, the group of administrative records may have natural subdivisions such as board meeting minutes or records relating to the creation and adoption of policies. Archival description encompasses the entirety of all of these groupings and their hierarchical relationships.

Function. Good archival description will discuss the *functions* of the individuals and organizations that created archival records, as well as the activities they undertook in the pursuit of those functions. Functions result in activities, which lead to the creation of documents; every document is the record of an activity that serves a particular function or functions. Although the idea of function is more explicitly dealt with in other countries, such as the United Kingdom, American archival theorist Theodore Schellenberg highlights the evidential value inherent in archival records—that is, the "evidence they contain of the organization and function of the Government body that produced them."[7] While the conceptual basis for describing function or activities emerged from the public archives tradition, there is also a sound basis for describing functions and activities of the people and families who create manuscripts or personal papers.

Archival Descriptive Standards

Tools used to describe archival materials have not always been constructed in a standard fashion; researchers could visit various archival institutions and encounter different descriptive formats and tools at each location. They would then not only have to learn how to use each finding aid but also could not expect to find the same information within each description. Even today, many repositories have legacy finding aids and other descriptive instruments that do not comply with the latest professional standards. It is important to understand the history of the development of archival descriptive standards in order to be familiar with the types of descriptive tools one may find within archival repositories and to understand the challenges archivists faced as they moved to standardize description. Some of the standards described below, namely MARC AMC, AACR2, and APPM, provide this historical background, even though they have been superseded by newer archival descriptive standards.

Archivists have long realized that applying standards to archival description would greatly increase discoverability of archival materials. Standards for archival description date to 1888, when Justin Winsor developed cataloging rules for manuscripts in the United States at the Massachusetts Historical Society.[8] However, before networked computers provided automated retrieval functionality, the development of archival descriptive standards at a national level was costly and time-consuming. One of the original purposes of standardizing archival description was to bring multiple descriptions together in one place for researchers to access. As discovered by the authors of the *National Union Catalog of Manuscript Collections*

---

7 Theodore Schellenberg, "The Appraisal of Modern Public Records," cited in the definition of "evidential value" in Pearce-Moses, *Glossary*.
8 Working Group on Standards for Archival Description, "Archival Description Standards: Report of the Working Group on Standards for Archival Description," *American Archivist* 52 (Fall 1989): 441.

(NUCMC), a print catalog of collection-level archival descriptions, this collation was difficult to maintain in a print environment due to the high number of records and the need for constant revisions. The advent of online catalogs, such as the national bibliographic utilities provided by the Research Libraries Information Network (RLIN) and the Online Computer Library Center (OCLC),[9] spurred archivists to standardize their description to take advantage of the increased visibility and access these catalogs could provide to archival materials.[10]

To understand the development of archival descriptive standards, it helps to review the different types of standards that are used to capture, describe, and even transmit data about archival collections. Many of these standards complement and can be used in conjunction with each other. Standards supporting archival description may be grouped into four categories: (1) data structure standards, (2) data content standards, (3) data value standards, and (4) metadata/companion standards.

Data Structure Standards

Data structure standards define what types of data elements may be found in a description and outline how the data elements relate to one another. For example, a structure standard may state that the data field "subject" can be included in a descriptive record, and that particular data field may include an attribute for "authority." In the relationship set by the standard, the attribute is a description of the data within the "subject" field, and the "subject" field itself serves to describe the object that is the subject of the descriptive record.[11] Data structure standards also may impose constraints on the data, for example, by imposing rules requiring the presence of particular data elements. Descriptive records created using the same data structure standard are interoperable: they are made with the understanding that records

---

9 In the early 1980s, the Research Libraries Group (RLG) expanded its nationally available bibliographic network (RLIN) to include descriptions of archival materials. OCLC soon followed.

10 A more detailed history of the development of archival descriptive standards is covered elsewhere. For a history of development of standards up to 1989, see Working Group on Standards for Archival Description, "Archival Description Standards: Report of the Working Group on Standards for Archival Description," *American Archivist* (Fall 1989): 431–537. See also Pitti, "Encoded Archival Description."

11 In this example, taken from the Metadata Object Description Schema (MODS) standard, the authority attribute details from which data value standard (described below) the subject term was selected.

created in one system will work with those created in another system. In this way, data structure standards make it possible to compile data records from various institutions and to build tools that search across them. Data structure standards are also platform neutral. They are not tied to a specific hardware- or software-computing platform, so even if newer technologies are developed, the descriptive records will not become obsolete. Following is a discussion of several standards that fall into this category.

Machine-Readable Cataloging (MARC) Records

The MARC format is a data structure standard developed by librarians in the 1960s to organize the information needed to describe bibliographic materials. The MARC format consists of a record composed of data elements, or categories of information, such as title, author, date, and subject.[12] Breaking individual records into data elements identifies the different components of the record, enabling actions on them, such as displaying, searching, or sorting the records. The MARC record format is also platform neutral, allowing continued use of the records even as technology changes.

MARC was originally created to provide access to print materials. One significant advantage of standardizing description using the MARC format was that librarians could reproduce descriptive information previously created by other libraries, a practice known as copy cataloging. This advantage did not apply to archival materials, which are unique in nature and require original description and cataloging. Thus, the efficiency of copy cataloging helped spur adoption of the MARC format among libraries, but it did not have the same effect on archives. The MARC format, composed of both fixed and variable-length fields with limited character length, was also not flexible or detailed enough for encapsulating the context of archival materials, which often requires detailed notes, descriptions of provenance, and information concerning the hierarchy of materials within a collection.

In the early 1980s the National Information Systems Task Force (NISTF), a group appointed by SAA, created a version of MARC specifically for describing archival materials. Called the MARC Format

---

12 Lisa B. Weber, "Record Formatting: MARC AMC," in *Describing Archival Materials: The Use of the MARC AMC Format*, ed. Richard P. Smiraglia (New York: Haworth Press, 1990), 118.

for Archival and Manuscripts Control (MARC AMC), this system later became the MARC Format for Archives and Mixed Collections.[13] At that time special MARC record formats were being created for a variety of different types of materials—serials, maps, visual materials, and computer files. It made sense to include a format for archival materials as well, to take advantage of the technology for the online catalogs of MARC records that was already developed, widely adopted, and familiar to researchers. The benefit of enabling researchers to use one system to discover print, archival, and other materials was considered worth the trade-off of losing some of the intricacy of archival description. The MARC AMC record provided a generalized description of an archival collection and included name and subject index terms as well as a note field indicating the availability of a finding aid or index in the repository. After finding the MARC record in an online catalog, the researcher would either request a copy of the printed finding aid or arrange a visit to view the finding aid and the corresponding collection. The data elements in a MARC AMC record also mapped directly to information captured by NUCMC entries, so that NUCMC records could be converted to AMC records.

There were many versions of MARC developed before MARC AMC, and development continued after its release. In 1998, MARBI, an interdivisional committee of the American Library Association (ALA); ALCTS (Association for Library Collections and Technical Services); LITA (Library and Information Technology Association); and RUSA (Reference and User Services Association), voted to return to a single integrated MARC record, rather than maintaining separate records for different types of formats.[14] In 1999, MARC 21, a format merging the U.S. MARC format and the Canadian MARC format, was

---

13 Working Group on Standards for Archival Description, "Report," 447. For a description of the work of the National Information Systems Task Force (NISTF), see Richard H. Lytle, "A National Information System for Archives and Manuscript Collections," *American Archivist* 43 (Summer 1980): 423–426; David Bearman, "Toward National Information Systems for Archives and Manuscript Repositories," *American Archivist* 45 (Winter 1982): 53–56; and Richard H. Lytle, "An Analysis of the Work of the National Information Systems Task Force," *American Archivist* 47 (Fall 1984): 357–365.
14 Working Group on Standards for Archival Description, *Standards for Archival Description: A Handbook,* comp. by Victoria Irons Walch (Chicago: Society of America Archivists, 1994), chap. 13, accessed August 17, 2012, http://www.archivists.org/catalog/stds99/chapter13.html.

adopted.[15] MARC 21 has also been adapted for use on the Web; an XML schema is available for MARC data (see Figure 2).

> **Figure 2. eXtensible Markup Language (XML)**
>
> Many data structure standards listed here are defined in eXtensible Markup Language (XML). XML is based on Standard Generalized Markup Language (SGML) and is a standard markup language for the World Wide Web. A markup language "is a set of tags and/or a set of rules for creating tags that can be embedded in digital text to provide additional information about the text in order to facilitate automated processing of it."[16] XML is used to encode the semantics of the data within a document and is also used for defining data structures. In this way XML is a standard for data exchange that, unlike the original MARC format,[17] is widely used outside of libraries, archives, and museums. XML provides a great deal of flexibility in data manipulation and transformation. The development of XML has resulted in many related technologies, such as XML schemas (XSD), which define tags (also known as elements) as well as their relationships to other elements, and XSLT, or eXtensible Stylesheet Language Transformation, which transforms XML into other formats, like HTML. Each element may be further refined by the use of attributes or by nesting refining elements within the parent element. Both attributes and refining elements are shown in Figures 3 and 4.[18] The structure of XML allows for the encoding of complex hierarchical information, which lends itself easily to archival description; elements can be nested inside one another in the same manner in which a series is nested in a collection, a subseries nested within a series, and a file nested within the subseries. The flexibility of XML led to its adoption as the encoding means for several different metadata standards that are discussed in the following sections, such as Encoded Archival Description (EAD). XML documents such as EAD files can be validated against rules established in a Document Type Definition (DTD) or an XML schema; current best practice is to validate against a schema.

---

15 *MARC 21 Bibliographic Introduction* (Washington, DC: Library of Congress, 2006), accessed August 17, 2012, http://www.loc.gov/marc/bibliographic/bdintro.html.
16 The Linux Information Project, *Markup Language Definition,* last updated May 30, 2006, accessed August 17, 2012, http://www.linfo.org/markup_language.html.
17 MARC is now also encoded in XML (MARCXML).
18 For a discussion of differences between attributes and refining elements, see "XML Attributes," http://w3schools.com/Xml/xml_attributes.asp.

24 ARCHIVAL ARRANGEMENT AND DESCRIPTION

Encoded Archival Description (EAD)

As Internet technology developed, archivists sought to transcend the limitations of the MARC AMC format, most notably its restrictive character length and inability to capture hierarchical relationships. They searched for ways to leverage new technologies to increase the amount and type of archival information accessible on the Internet. Archival institutions wanted to place entire finding aids online, not just collection descriptions in catalogs. In 1997, Encoded Archival Description, or EAD, was released as the first data structure standard created by the archival community. It is now the most commonly used standard for encoding finding aids. The current version of the standard was updated in 2002.[19] EAD is currently undergoing a process of revision by the Technical Subcommittee on Encoded Archival Description (TS-EAD) of the Society of American Archivists.[20]

EAD was the result of a series of projects at major universities, governmental repositories, and professional organizations, as well as archivists who lent their time, their expertise, and their finding aids toward this goal.[21] Testing began with the alpha release of the standard in early 1996, and the public release later that year led to additional projects initiated and funded by granting agencies with the production of EAD finding aids as a goal. These projects aimed to use standardized description to compile finding aids in consortium-based databases, with a single search interface for users, or to index digital objects—goals that are now common practice at many institutions.

Data structure standards like EAD preserve the hierarchical structure of information within a collection in a simple and standardized fashion. When developing this standard, the archivists involved sought to find a middle ground between best practice and common practice. Janice Ruth, a member of the EAD development team, recalled: "Concerned that it not create an overly enforcing, prescriptive, or burdensome DTD,[22] the

---

19 Documentation of the standard is maintained by the Network Development and MARC Standards Office at the Library of Congress. See Library of Congress, Encoded Archival Description Tag Library—Version 2002, http://www.loc.gov/ead/tglib/.
20 The description of two elements in the following section (particularly changes to the <eadheader> and the absence of <dsc>) conforms to proposed changes presented by the TS-EAD at the Encoded Archival Description Roundtable meeting at the Society of American Archivists' Annual Meeting on August 8, 2012.
21 Pitti, "Encoded Archival Description," 279–281.
22 EAD was originally devised as an XML DTD. After XML schema languages (a newer technology than DTDs) developed, EAD was updated in schema form.

team decided to mandate the use of few elements and allowed for the nesting and reuse of elements to capture 'progressively more detailed and specific levels of description as desired.'"[23]

The 2002 version of the EAD tag library lists 146 separate elements, providing a definition and description of each. Each definition includes information on:

- the nature of the element (what type of data it should contain, such as a biography or history of the collection's creator);
- what kinds of elements may be nested within the element being defined, and what kinds of elements it may be nested within;
- what attributes a specific element may be associated with (that is, for example, the "type" or "label" of a particular element);
- examples of each element;
- crosswalks to ISAD(G) and MARC 21, if applicable; and
- whether a particular element is required for a valid EAD document.

As long as an EAD document includes the required elements specified in the EAD schema, it is considered valid. The use of most elements is optional, allowing institutions to choose appropriate levels of granularity for their encoding. Each element may contain additional elements or attributes that allow portions of each note to be nested within tags that describe the text within. For example, each time a personal name occurs within the text of a <scopecontent> element, the name may be surrounded by a <persname> tag to signify that the text represents the name of a person. This enables systems to conduct more detailed indexing and searching of the EAD document. The EAD schema allows this practice but does not mandate it. Personal names may also be entered in the <controlaccess> element, which is a wrapper element that contains descriptive access points that may conform to various controlled vocabularies, such as the Library of Congress Name Authority File (LCNAF), described below. Personal names might not be tagged at all. EAD provides the ability to encode description to a level that suits a particular repository's practice and method of discovery.

Major Sections Within an EAD Document. An EAD document is

---

[23] Janice Ruth, "Encoded Archival Description: A Structural Overview," *American Archivist* 60 (Summer 1997): 314.

contained within the root element <ead>, which holds two sections: the <eadheader> and the <archdesc>.

<eadheader>[24]

The <eadheader> element is the first required element within the <ead> root element and contains information about the finding aid document, such as author and date of publication. It serves as a wrapper element—the only data it contains lie within other nested elements. Elements contained within <eadheader> are:

- **<eadid>** (required): provides a unique identifier for the EAD document, including references to the country and repository where the EAD document is maintained;
- **<filedesc>** (required): contains the <titlestmt> element that transmits the title of the finding aid and author information;
- **<profiledesc>**: contains information about the encoded version of the finding aid (which may differ from information about the non-encoded version); and
- **<revisiondesc>**: contains information about revisions made to the encoded version of the finding aid.

<archdesc>

The <archdesc> element is a required element that provides information about the archival materials. It is a wrapper element that contains elements that describe the collection at different levels. Information contained at the top level of description within this element is connected to—literally wrapped around—lower levels of description, which accords with archival organization and practice. This practice also saves archivists time; rather than retyping description at every level of a finding aid, description encoded at the top level will apply to subordinate levels of organization. Many elements may occur within the <archdesc>:[25]

> **<did>:** The descriptive identification element, or <did>, must be the first element listed with the <archdesc>. It is also a wrapper element that contains other elements and attributes

---

24 Proposed changes to EAD indicate that the <eadheader> element will be replaced by a <control> element, which would align EAD more closely with other archival XML-based standards, such as EAC-CPF (discussed below).

25 The <dsc> element is on the list for proposed deprecation and is thus not discussed in this document.

that describe the collection as a whole. Elements within the <did> at the <archdesc> level may include information customarily included in a collection-level description or MARC record for an archival collection. These include:
- <origination>, creator/collector name;
- <unittitle>, collection name;
- <physdesc>, a wrapper element that can include format, container, and extent;[26] and
- .

Descriptive notes: Following the <did>, the <archdesc> contains elements for additional information describing the materials at the collection level. Examples of these notes include:
- <accessrestrict>, restrictions governing access;
- <arrangement>, arrangement of the materials;
- <bioghist>, biographical or historical note;
- <processinfo>, processing information;
- <scopecontent>, scope and content note; and
- <controlaccess>, subject headings for the collection.[27]

<c>: Description of subordinate levels of the collection is communicated through <c>, or component, elements. Each of these <c> elements describes a level of the collection subordinate to the one that contains it. For example, description of a subseries is nested within description of a series. Additionally, <c> elements may be numbered to distinguish which elements are subordinate to which parent. A <c01> may contain one or more <c02> elements, where <c01> is a series (so designated by the element's LEVEL attribute) and <c02> a subseries, with various <c03> file-level components contained within it. Most of the elements that are permissible within the <archdesc> component are also permissible within various <c> elements.[28] Figure 3 provides an example of the proper usage of <c> elements. Figures 3 and 4 provide usage examples for component description and the <persname> element.

---

26 This element is slated to become more structured in the proposed revision.
27 A full list of the elements that may currently be nested within <archdesc> may be found at http://www.loc.gov/ead/tglib/elements/archdesc.html.
28 A full list of the elements that may currently be nested within a <c> element may be found at http://www.loc.gov/ead/tglib/elements/c.html.

Figure 3. Example of <c01> and <c02> Tags with Other Descriptive Elements

```
<c01 level="series">
  <did>
    <unittitle>Early Career</unittitle>
    <unitid>1</unitid>
    <physdesc>
      <extent>1.3 cubic ft.</extent>
    </physdesc>
    <unitdate normal="1944/1959" type="inclusive">
    1944-1959</unitdate>
  </did>
  <scopecontent>
    <head>Scope and Contents note</head>
    <p>This series consists of correspondence, class
    notes, research notes, and manuscripts relating to
    Knowles' undergraduate and graduate training, and
    to his research in diseases of the heart and lungs
    at Portsmouth Naval Hospital, as a United States
    Public Health Service fellow, and as intern and
    resident at Massachusetts General Hospital.</p>
  </scopecontent>
  <arrangement>
    <head>Arrangement note</head>
      <p>This series is arranged by subject and
      chronologically within each subject.</p>
  </arrangement>
  <c02 level="file">
    <did>
      <unittitle>Correspondence</unittitle>
      <container id="cid5615277" type="Box"
      label="Mixed materials">1 </container>
      <container parent="cid5615277" type="Folder">
      1</container>
      <unitdate normal="1944/1955" type="inclusive">
      1944-1955</unitdate>
    </did>
  </c02>
  <c02 level="file">
    <did>
      <unittitle>Harvard - Class Notes</unittitle>
      <container id="cid5615276" type="Box"
      label="Mixed materials">1</container>
```

```
            <container parent="cid5615276" type="Folder">
            2</container>
        </did>
    </c02>
</c01>
```

Source: Rockefeller Archive Center, *A Guide to the John H. Knowles Papers*, accessed October 11, 2012, http://collectionguides.rockarch.org/xtf/view?docID=ead/FA047/FA047.xml.

Figure 4. Examples of <persname>

Example of <persname> within <scopecontent>
```
<scopecontent id="ref7">
  <head>Scope and Contents note</head>
  <p>Includes biographical material, bibliographic
  material, clippings, correspondence, and
  photographs.</p>
  <p>Correspondents include <persname>Rufus Cole
  </persname>, <persname>Herbert
  Gasser</persname>, <persname>Edric Smith</persname>,
  and <persname>Donald D. Van Slyke</persname>.</p>
</scopecontent>
```

Example of <persname> within <controlaccess>
```
<controlaccess>
    <persname rules="dacs">Bergmann, Martha</persname>
    <corpname source="lcnaf">United States. Armed
    Forces.</corpname>
    <subject source="lcsh">Biochemistry</subject>
    <subject source="lcsh">Chemical warfare</subject>
    <geogname source="lcsh">Japan</geogname>
    <subject source="lcsh">World War II</subject>
</controlaccess>
```

Source: Above: Rockefeller Archive Center, *A Guide to the Homer F. Swift, Rockefeller University Faculty Papers*, accessed October 11, 2012, http://collectionguides.rockarch.org/xtf/view?docID=ead/FA201/FA201.xml. Below: Rockefeller Archive Center, *A Guide to the Max Bergmann, Rockefeller University Faculty Papers*, accessed October 11, 2012, http://collectionguides.rockarch.org/xtf/view?docID=ead/FA001/FA001.xml. In this example, "source" is an attribute of <subject> that explains from which controlled vocabulary the content of the element ("Chemical warfare") was selected.

EAD Adoption. Creating a data standard that adheres to common practices of archival description is one thing; convincing archivists to use the standard is another. In the fifteen years since its creation, EAD has become widely seen as a standard that all repositories should adopt. However, not all repositories have implemented it; in a 2008 study, nearly 50 percent of respondents reported that they had not adopted the standard.[29] Not all archivists have knowledge of XML or the ability to provide support for computer programs that will convert their existing descriptions (in whatever electronic or analog format they may be) into an XML file. Other repositories may not have any staff who possess knowledge about how to configure a server to host and display EAD finding aids. An OCLC Research report published in 2010 discusses these barriers to EAD implementation and provides suggestions on how to overcome them.[30]

EAD defines many elements that can capture a great deal of information, and repositories have to make decisions about not only which elements to encode but also how to encode them. *Describing Archives: A Content Standard* (DACS), described later in this module, provides guidance on the completion of EAD elements, but except for a few elements, it does not require their use. Many archives have found it necessary to include EAD-specific instructions in their processing guides. Such guides may provide detailed instructions on local practices, such as how to nest <c> elements, in order to standardize the finding aids within the institution.

Encoded Archival Context—Corporate Bodies, Persons, and Families (EAC-CPF)

EAC-CPF, which is encoded as an XML schema, serves as a framework for communicating descriptive information about the individuals, groups, and institutions that create, collect, preserve, and are the subject of archival collections. EAC-CPF is designed to support the sharing of authority records and linking of archival collections in disparate repositories. SAA adopted it as a standard in 2011, and it is maintained by SAA's EAC Working Group.[31]

---

29 "AT User Group Survey Results: Proposed New Features and Functionality," Archivists' Toolkit, 2008, p. 2, accessed August 20, 2012, http://archiviststoolkit.org/sites/default/files/AT%20User%20Group%20SurveyResultsFD.pdf.
30 Michele Combs et al., *Over, Under, Around, and Through: Getting Around Barriers to EAD Implementation.* Dublin, OH: OCLC Research, 2010. Published online at http://www.oclc.org/research/publications/library/2010/2010-04.pdf.
31 *Encoded Archival Context—Corporate Bodies, Persons, and Families (EAC-CPF) Tag Library,* version 2010, accessed August 16, 2012, http://www3.iath.virginia.edu/eac/cpf/tagLibrary/cpfTagLibrary.html. For additional information, see Dennis Meissner and Jennifer Schaffner, "Introducing EAC-CPF," *Archival Outlook* (May/June 2010): 10–11, http://www2.archivists.org/sites/all/files/AO-MayJun2010.pdf.

The advent of EAD, and the possibilities it presented for expressing, sharing, and linking structured information about collections, opened the door for the creation of EAC-CPF—a standard used to express, share, and link information about the creators of archival materials. Such archival authority records relate closely to bibliographic authority records but contain more detailed and more complex information about the context of creators.

Rationale for EAC-CPF. Initial efforts to define a content standard for archival authority records were undertaken by ICA, which released the first edition of the International Standard Archival Authority Record (Corporate Bodies, Persons, and Families) (ISAAR[CPF]) in 1996.[32] Two years later, work began in the United States to develop a standard to encode ISAAR(CPF)-compliant archival authority records. EAC-CPF was released as a beta version in 2004.[33]

Communicating the context within which archival creators operated aids in understanding more completely the archival materials themselves. Maintaining separate archival authority records and liberating creator descriptions from within individual finding aids allows data to be linked in ways not previously possible (individual to individual, or individual to multiple collections, for example, rather than simply collection to individual, or collection to collection). Recording authority records and other contextual information outside of records describing the content of the records also saves time and improves access. For example, a university archives could use EAC-CPF to record an administrative history for a campus office, then link that history to multiple EAD files.[34]

EAC-CPF also allows archivists to specify *how* entities are related, not merely *that* they are related. For example, while many users may be aware that John F. Kennedy and Jacqueline Bouvier Kennedy were married, or that John F. Kennedy served as the president of the United States, not all users would be aware of the relationship between John F.

---

32 Katherine M. Wisser, "Describing Entities and Identities: The Development and Structure of Encoded Archival Context—Corporate Bodies, Persons, and Families," *Journal of Library Metadata* 11, no. 3–4 (2011): 167.

33 *Encoded Archival Context—Corporate Bodies, Persons, and Families (EAC-CPF) Tag Library.* See also International Council on Archives, Committee on Descriptive Standards, *ISAAR(CPF): International Standard Archival Authority Record for Corporate Bodies, Persons, and Families,* 2nd ed., p. 8, http://www.icacds.org/uk/eng/ISAAR(CPF)2ed.pdf.

34 "Background," *Encoded Archival Context—Corporate Bodies, Persons, and Families (EAC-CPF) Tag Library.*

Kennedy and John Bartlow Martin[35] (Martin, who won accolades for his biography of Adlai Stevenson, served as a staff member on Kennedy's 1960 presidential campaign) or the book *Profiles in Courage* (which Kennedy authored). Any of these relationships could be expressed via EAC-CPF. Archivists gain a valuable perspective by looking at description as a holistic effort undertaken across repositories and geographic boundaries, engaged in describing entities that themselves operated across geographic and professional boundaries.[36] Users also gain valuable knowledge by tracing these connections to other entities and archival collections.

Like EAD, EAC-CPF defines a variety of elements and attributes that may be employed to describe the persons, corporate bodies, and families that constitute the context of archival records. Also like EAD, a subset of the elements is required to create a valid EAC-CPF record. Most elements and attributes are optional, meaning that each repository may modify use of these elements and attributes to suit local practice. Even optional elements and attributes have rules regarding how and where in each record they may be used.

Major Sections Within an EAC-CPF Record. An EAC-CPF document is contained in the root element <eac-cpf>. Within that root element, two subordinate, or child, elements are required: <control> and <cpfDescription>. Both are wrapper elements that contain other elements.

<control>
The <control> element describes how, by whom, and according to what standards and practices (international, national, and local) the entity authority record was created—in short, it is about the authority record itself. Six subordinate elements are required; five are optional.

---

35 A search for Kennedy in the prototype version of the Social Networks and Archival Context Project (SNAC) revealed this connection (and that Kennedy and Martin corresponded); the biographical note and contents listed in the finding aid for Martin's papers at the Library of Congress explained Martin's role that connected the two. Accessed August 19, 2012, http://memory.loc.gov/service/mss/eadxmlmss/eadpdfmss/2003/ms003018.pdf and http://socialarchive.iath.virginia.edu/xtf/view?docId=kennedy-john-f-john-fitzgerald-1917-1963-cr.xml.

36 As the authors of ISAAR(CPF) point out, the creation of archival materials is itself increasingly international in nature: "The multinational character of past and present record keeping creates the incentive for international standardization which will support the exchange of contextual information. For example, processes such as colonialization, immigration and trade have contributed to the multinational character of recordkeeping." International Council on Archives, *ISAAR(CPF): International Standard Archival Authority Record for Corporate Bodies, Persons, and Families,* 8.

For example, the subordinate <recordID> element contains a unique identifier for each authority record; this element is required.[37] Also required is the <maintenanceAgency> element, which contains information about the institution responsible for the creation and management of the EAC-CPF record and which has two children elements: <agencyCode> and <agencyName>. The combination of the code provided in <agencyCode> and the identifier in <recordID> can be used as a globally unique identifier for the EAC-CPF instance.[38] For a full list of required and optional elements within the <control> element, see the *EAC-CPF Tag Library*.[39]

<cpfDescription>
The <cpfDescription> element contains the entity description, or content, of the authority record. One subordinate element is required; others are optional.[40]

> **<identity>:** The required subordinate element is the <identity> element, which contains required and optional subordinate elements. This element contains the names of the entity, which may include names that change over time, especially for corporate bodies (such as a particular administrative office) or name changes due to marriages or mergers. Subordinate elements allow the archivist to indicate which name is the authorized or primary name for the record.
>
> **<description>:** An optional subordinate element is the <description> element, which contains a series of optional subordinate elements that allow for robust description of the instance, including elements that describe the function and mandate of the entity, its dates of existence or operation, a biography or administrative history of the entity, and genealogical information about the entity. Many of these elements represent information that archivists commonly collect about creators or subjects of collections.

---

37 See also Wisser, "Describing Entities and Identities," 170.
38 *Encoded Archival Context—Corporate Bodies, Persons, and Families (EAC-CPF) Tag Library*.
39 Ibid.
40 See *EAC-CPF Tag Library* and Wisser, "Describing Entities and Identities," 170–172.

<relations>: This is an optional subordinate element that allows for direct linkages between different entities, functions or actions, and archival materials. Linking people and organizations to each other, to activities and actions, and to other archival materials creates a web of connections that can be manipulated and sorted by a computer or even represented visually.[41] The <relations> element includes three subordinate elements:

- <cpfRelation>, which, with its attributes, communicates the type of relation specified to another corporate body, person, or family (example: parent of);
- <functionRelation>, which, with its attributes, communicates a relationship to a particular function or activity undertaken by the subject of the authority record (example: owns); and
- <resourceRelation>, which, with its attributes, communicates how an identity relates to an archival resource or another resource, such as a book or museum object (example: creator of).

<multipleIdentities>
The <multipleIdentities> element allows for multiple <cpfDescription> elements within a single descriptive instance. Rather than creating separate records for John F. Kennedy, Navy lieutenant; John F. Kennedy, U.S. senator; and John F. Kennedy, U.S. president, and subsequently linking them, all three identities could be bundled in one EAC-CPF record. Instances can be linked to one or more entities, and repositories can decide which number of links works best given their circumstances and implementation strategy.

Like the EAD tag library, the EAC-CPF tag library contains a list of elements arranged alphabetically. The list specifies the precise rules by which a particular element operates. For example, it specifies when an element may occur within another element, lists valid refining/child elements, and specifies element attributes.[42]

---

41 As the authors of the tag library explain, "Because relations occur between the descriptive nodes, they are most efficiently created and maintained outside of each node. A person, for example, can be related to one or more persons, organizations or families; to one or more archival records, books, journals, and museum objects; and to various occupations and activities." *Encoded Archival Context—Corporate Bodies, Persons, and Families (EAC-CPF) Tag Library.*

42 *Encoded Archival Context—Corporate Bodies, Persons, and Families (EAC-CPF) Tag Library.*

Data Content Standards

In addition to standards that regulate the *structure* of data, there are also standards that regulate the *content* of data. Content standards describe how content should be expressed. For example, *Describing Archives: A Content Standard* (DACS) provides people who describe archival collections with a series of rules that guide description and how to derive titles and form the names of the people and organizations associated with collections.

Data content standards also ask that archivists input information within the fields delineated in data structure standards in the same way across collections, repositories, and even institutions. Consistent application of standards allows for complete indexing and discovery of materials with similar content.

Many, though not all, archival data content standards are *format neutral*. Format-neutral standards can be used to describe any type of records, from parchment scrolls to e-mail messages. Other data content standards focus on the description of a particular group of materials, such as manuscripts or graphic materials.

Archival data content standards are also *output neutral*, which means, for example, that DACS-compliant description can exist whether the finding aid data is ultimately encoded as XML, mapped into database fields, or captured as simple text. Adopting data content standards does not necessitate adopting data structure standards, but doing so will both create more consistent and thorough description and prepare a repository to migrate its description to a data structure standard in the future. Following is a discussion of a number of standards in this category.

Anglo-American Cataloging Rules (AACR)

The MARC AMC data structure standard provided data elements for the encoding of archival descriptions, but it did not specify how the content within the data elements should be completed. After a series of precursor rules and guidelines for cataloging, the Anglo-American Cataloging Rules (AACR), a data content standard that provides guidance for the completion of MARC bibliographic elements, was published in 1967. This standard stood, with occasional revisions, until 1978, when a second version (AACR2) was published.[43] AACR2

---
43 Joint Steering Committee for the Development of RDA, *A Brief History of AACR*, July 1, 2009, accessed August 20, 2012, http://www.rda-jsc.org/history.html.

has remained the predominant library cataloging standard through several revisions. However, a new standard, Resource Description and Access (RDA), was published by the ALA in 2010. The Library of Congress has announced its intention to become RDA-compliant, and most other libraries are expected to follow.[44]

Archives, Personal Papers, and Manuscripts (APPM)

Although AACR2 was sufficient in meeting the needs of the library community, archivists thought it was inadequate for archival description, especially for describing entire collections of archival materials. AACR2 contains a chapter on manuscripts, but it focuses on cataloging single manuscript items, not collections. To fill this gap, Steven L. Hensen created *Archives, Personal Papers, and Manuscripts* (APPM), a guide for the content creation of MARC AMC records. APPM is considered the first archival content standard. APPM is largely based on AACR2, yet it recognizes three principles AACR2 overlooks: the importance of provenance in archival description, the need for collection-level rather than item-level bibliographic control, and the fact that archival materials are often kept for reasons other than the ones behind their creation.[45]

The adoption of MARC AMC and APPM by the archival community signaled a major step in the profession's involvement in the creation and implementation of standards for archival description. This venture was significant in that it represented a widespread agreement in the profession that archival description could, in some fashion, be standardized. Archival materials may be unique, but the descriptions that provide access to them can be conveyed in a standardized fashion. Although the MARC format had significant limitations, its success in increasing access to archival collections inspired the archival community to tackle the challenge of providing online access to standardized finding aids. In 1982 the SAA Council committed the society to the maintenance and support of MARC AMC, solidifying the profession's support of the standard,[46] although changes to the AMC format must be submitted to MARBI.

---

44 American Library Association et al., *Resource, Description and Access Toolkit*, accessed September 25, 2012, http://www.rdatoolkit.org/.
45 Steven L. Hensen, "The First Shall Be First: APPM and Its Impact on Archival Description," *Archivaria* 35 (Spring 1993): 64–70.
46 Working Group on Standards for Archival Description, "Report," 447.

General International Standard Archival Description (ISAD[G])

The MARC AMC and APPM standards were developed and implemented mainly by U.S.-based archives. The International Council on Archives (ICA), a nongovernmental organization that works to promote the preservation and use of archives across the globe, has developed several standards relating to the description of archival materials, including the General International Standard Archival Description, or ISAD(G).

ISAD(G) is a content standard created by the ICA Ad Hoc Commission on Descriptive Standards and was adopted by ICA in 1993.[47] A second edition of the standard was adopted in 1999. Modeled on the international library community's General International Standard for Bibliographic Description (ISBD[G]), it provides general guidance for the preparation of descriptions of archival materials.[48] ISAD(G) is used in conjunction with existing national standards and as the basis for the development of new national standards.[49] Because it is designed for use with other standards, ISAD(G) does not specify a record format or cataloging rules; rather, it sets out four principles for multilevel archival description and twenty-six data elements for use within an archival catalog, only six of which are considered essential for international exchange of descriptive information.[50]

The four principles of multilevel archival description are:

1. Description proceeds from the general to the specific.
2. Only information relevant to the level of the unit being described should be provided.
3. Levels of description should be linked.
4. To avoid redundancy, information should be listed only at the highest applicable unit of description.[51]

ISAD(G) has been widely adopted throughout the world and serves as the foundation of several national archival descriptive

---

47 International Council on Archives, Committee on Descriptive Standards, "History of ICA/CDS," accessed August 20, 2012, http://www.icacds.org.uk/eng/history.htm.
48 Working Group on Standards for Archival Description, *Standards for Archival Description*, chap. 13, accessed August 20, 2012, http://www.archivists.org/catalog/stds99/chapter13.html.
49 International Council on Archives, *ISAD(G): General International Standard Archival Description*, 7.
50 The six elements essential for international exchange of descriptive information are reference code, title, creator, date(s), extent of the unit of description, and level of description. *ISAD(G): General International Standard Archival Description*, 9.
51 *ISAD(G): General International Standard Archival Description*, 12.

38 ARCHIVAL ARRANGEMENT AND DESCRIPTION

standards, such as DACS in the United States and the Rules for Archival Description (RAD) in Canada.

Describing Archives: A Content Standard (DACS)

DACS is the data content standard for archival description within the United States. The standard was adopted by SAA in 2004 and is currently undergoing a process of revision, which is to be completed in 2013.

DACS grew out of efforts in the mid-1990s to revise APPM. As mentioned earlier, APPM guided the creation of MARC catalog records for collections, which were limited in size and tailored to the needs of cataloging systems. The development of EAD, which provided an opportunity to encode entire finding aids online, opened the door for a more comprehensive descriptive standard.[52]

DACS gives detailed instructions on how content should be formulated within specific descriptive elements, including notes and access points. These instructions are founded on a series of principles, based on ISAD(G), that posit arrangement and description as actions that stem from the inherently hierarchical organization of archival materials. DACS is equipped to discuss description at any level of arrangement; it can be used for description at the item level as well as for description at the collection level.

DACS also incorporates flexibility into its descriptive rules. First, while the standard complies with ISAD(G), it also provides room for local practices as well as the usage of other standards. Second, while DACS mandates the inclusion of certain elements for compliant description at various levels, it does not suggest that all elements should be included in descriptions of all collections or even that a repository use a particular non-required element in descriptions of all of its collections.[53]

DACS is currently divided into three parts: describing archival materials, describing creators, and forming names. The section on forming names is slated for elimination in the next version, and it will not be discussed in this module.[54]

---

52 *Describing Archives: A Content Standard* (Chicago: Society of American Archivists, 2007), v–vii.
53 *Describing Archives: A Content Standard*, 9–12.
54 *Describing Archives: A Content Standard*, "Statement of Principles," xv.

The first section is further broken down into seven groups of elements (Chapters 2–8); each group centers on elements with related content. Within each group, elements are numbered as extensions of the group number; for example, Chapter 2 focuses on identity elements (or elements that contain information about the identity of the repository, the collection, and the creator/collector), and the seven elements in that chapter are numbered 2.1 through 2.7.

Within each chapter, each element is defined and its purpose explained. Most elements are also further subdivided to include rules governing the content of the element, including sources from which the information contained within each element may be found. Many elements also list exclusions, or types of content that should be not be included in a particular note, that aid in determining which notes should be used for which types of data. Element 5.1, which focuses on custodial history, is not only defined (as "information on changes of ownership or custody of the material being described, from the time it left the possession of the creator until it was acquired by the repository, that is significant for its authenticity, integrity, and interpretation") but also distinguished from a related element ("Record information about the donor or source from which the archives directly acquired the unit being described in the Immediate Source of Acquisition Element [5.2].")[55]

DACS 2.3 defines the purpose of a collection title ("a word or phrase by which the material being described is known or can be identified") and explains how to devise, or compose, one. Generally, an archivist should combine the name of the creator/collector with a description of the nature of the materials. DACS then lists a series of examples for how different types of titles may be formed. The title for the papers of an individual (the John F. Kennedy Papers) would be formed differently from the records of an office (the Office of the President Records), which differ from a collection that centers on a particular subject (the Collection on the assassination of John F. Kennedy) or predominantly contains a particular type of materials (Lyndon B. Johnson Correspondence).

As mentioned above, data structure standards, such as EAD, and data content standards, such as DACS, were designed to be compatible

---

55 *Describing Archives: A Content Standard*, 77.

with each other. EAD provides the scaffolding to create hierarchical description, while DACS explains how to express that hierarchy. Thus, the example cited above would look something like this in EAD:

```
<archdesc>
    <did>
    ...
      <unittitle>John F. Kennedy papers</unittitle>
    ...
    </did>
</archdesc>
```

In this example there is a structure element in EAD that matches a data content area described in DACS. Most content items listed in DACS have direct EAD analogs, but not all do. Conservation notes, described in DACS 7.1.3, are intended to "[d]escribe any specific conservation treatment." There is no EAD tag that correlates to this specific action. The two closest tags are <processinfo> (any action taken to make materials available to researchers, and which can occur at any level of description within a finding aid) and <phystech> (anything that would affect a researcher's use of or access to a particular record, especially any equipment required for use or access). Archivists at a particular repository using both EAD and DACS will need to decide whether they will put conservation information in their finding aids and how they will use (or not use) <processinfo> and <phystech> elements in that description.

In the forthcoming revision of DACS, the second section will be expanded. It will focus on creating and employing archival authority records as an efficient and useful way both to identify and describe creators, collectors, and the context of archival materials and to link collections across repositories and institutions. Chapter 9 instructs archivists how to create a robust archival authority record for the creators and collectors represented in their collections. The chapter also usefully distinguishes between archival authority records and bibliographic authority records; the former seeks to capture the context of records creation, thus making it longer and more comprehensive than bibliographic authority records.[56]

The instructions in the DACS revision are in part drawn from the International Standard Archival Authority Record for Corporate

---

56 DACS Revision (proposed) (July 2012), 124–125, accessed September 25, 2012, http://www2.archivists.org/sites/all/files/DACS%20Revision%20%28July%202012%29.pdf.

Bodies, Persons, and Families (ISAAR[CPF]), an international descriptive standard described later in this module. The instructions also outline the required and suggested elements for inclusion in a compliant archival authority record. For example, a basic archival authority record for an individual requires four components: an authorized form of the name, entity type, dates, and an identifier for the authority record.

Several appendices augment the instructions provided in DACS. Some of these appendices point archivists toward other published resources, including Richard Pearce-Moses's *Glossary of Archival Terms*.[57] Others direct users to content standards that are more tailored to describing a particular type of archival materials, such as maps, graphic materials, or data sets; data value standards, such as LCNAF or the Getty Thesaurus of Geographic Names (TGN); or data structure standards, such as EAD. Still others provide crosswalks, or connections between elements with the same meaning or function, between DACS and other standards, such as MODS and Dublin Core.

International Standard Archival Authority Record for Corporate Bodies, Persons, and Families (ISAAR[CPF])

During the development of ISAD(G), the ICA Commission on Descriptive Standards realized that providing information on the creators of archival material was just as integral to archival description as the description of the material itself. The Commission thus charged a subgroup to develop a complementary content standard for archival authority records and published ISAAR(CPF) in 1996.[58] The second edition of the standard was adopted in 2003. Like ISAD(G), ISAAR(CPF) is designed to be used in conjunction with, or as the basis for the development of, national standards. EAC-CPF, described above, is a data structure standard based on the elements laid out in ISAAR(CPF).

Similar to library authority records, ISAAR(CPF) provides guidelines for capturing variant names and authorized access points. However, unlike bibliographic authority records, the purpose is to include information about the context within which archival materials

---

57 Pearce-Moses, *Glossary*.
58 International Council on Archives, Committee on Descriptive Standards, "History."

were generated. The standard is organized into four information areas that outline the elements of description for an archival authority record: the Identity Area, the Description Area, the Relationships Area, and the Control Area. The Identity Area provides information for the unique identification of an entity, including its variant forms of names. The Control Area captures data about the ISAAR(CPF) record itself, such as its unique identifier and the name of its creating agency. Both areas are similar to Identity and Control elements in bibliographic authority records. In the Description and Relationships Areas, the two types of authority records diverge. The Description Area is "where relevant information is conveyed about the nature, context, and activities of the entity being described."[59] This includes information concerning the history of the entity, the places in which the entity lived or did business, and even the genealogy of an entity. The Relationships Area is where information concerning the entity's relationships with other corporate bodies, persons, or families is recorded. This type of information is extremely valuable in providing linkages between records creators, as one ISAAR(CPF) description can link to many other ISAAR(CPF) descriptions, each of which may lead a researcher to potentially relevant archival materials.

International Standard for Describing Functions (ICA-ISDF)

The International Standard for Describing Functions (ICA-ISDF) is a content standard for capturing information about the functions performed by records creators that result in the creation of records. According to the standard, a function is "[a]ny high level purpose, responsibility or task assigned to the accountability agenda of a corporate body by legislation, policy or mandate."[60] The standard was approved by ICA in 2008. ICA-ISDF is interoperable with other international standards, like ISAAR(CPF), that describe records creators.

Functions can be used to identify and track business activities over time, even as agency names and responsibilities change. Description

---

59 International Council on Archives, *ISAAR(CPF): International Standard Archival Authority Record for Corporate Bodies, Persons, and Families*, 2nd ed., p. 13. Adopted by the Committee on Descriptive Standards, Canberra, Australia, October 27–30, 2003. Accessed August 20, 2012, http://www.icacds.org.uk/eng/ISAAR(CPF)2ed.pdf.
60 International Council on Archives, *ISDF: International Standard for Describing Functions*, p. 10. Adopted by the Committee of Best Practices and Standards (CBPS), Dresden, Germany, May 2–4, 2007. Accessed August 20, 2012, http://www.wien2004.ica.org/sites/default/files/ISDF%20ENG.pdf.

of functions can be linked to description of multiple administrative offices, rather than describing the function in each description of each agency. Additionally, information about functions can inform core archival practice, providing archivists information relevant to appraisal, arrangement, and access decisions.[61] Currently, there is no supporting data structure standard for ICA-ISDF.

International Standard for Describing Institutions with Archival Holdings (ICA-ISDIAH)

ICA promulgates a fourth related data content standard called the International Standard for Describing Institutions with Archival Holdings (ICA-ISDIAH). Published in 2008, ISDIAH is a standard method of providing descriptive information about the institutions at which archival materials are stored and may be accessed.[62] Like ISDF, ISDIAH is interoperable with other international standards, such as ISAAR(CPF). Much of the information codified in this standard is usually communicated in an institution's publications or website (for example, contact information, hours of operation, or services provided and their costs). Other information in this standard may not normally be communicated by most U.S. archival repositories, such as element 5.3.6 ("Buildings"), which includes information about the physical structures in which archives are held, including their storage capacity.[63]

As with ISDF, the description mandated by ISDIAH can be reused for related purposes. ISDIAH-compliant description can be compiled and used to create directories of repositories according to geographic location, type of institution, or services rendered; it can also allow both users and archivists to make connections between related institutions or institutions with related collections.[64] As with most standards, description that adheres to ISDIAH may be published or displayed in a variety of ways.[65]

---

61 Ibid., 7.
62 International Council on Archives, *ISDIAH: International Standard for Describing Institutions with Archival Holdings.* Developed by the Committee on Best Practices and Standards, London, UK, March 10–11, 2008. Accessed August 20, 2012, http://www.wien2004.ica.org/sites/default/files/ISDIAH%20Eng_0.pdf.
63 Ibid., 29–31.
64 Ibid., 9.
65 Ibid., 55.

Data Value Standards

Data structure standards provide a framework for encoding descriptive elements, and data content standards provide guidance on how to construct content for those elements. For some elements, however, the most appropriate content is derived from a *controlled vocabulary*, or a pre-specified set of terms. A controlled vocabulary that contains hierarchical relationships between terms is known as a *thesaurus*. Vocabularies and thesauri are types of data value standards and ensure that the same person, subject, or other value is consistently used across different types of description (archival, bibliographic, or other type of description) and different institutions. Terms from data value standards are used in archival description and are referred to as *controlled access headings*.

Data value standards may take the form of a flat list of terms, such as the Library of Congress subject headings (described below); a list of codes, such as ISO-639.2 (an ISO-created list of three-letter codes for languages); or a thesaurus, such as the Art and Architecture Thesaurus (described below). Data value standards facilitate searching for information within a library catalog because they standardize the data fields within which to search. Many of these standards (particularly those for names and subjects) were created by librarians to describe non-unique printed materials, such as books, serials, and other publications. Data value standards promote the use of one preferred term over all of its potential synonyms. Non-preferred terms are often listed in the standard as a "See" reference, pointing to the preferred term. Following are examples of data value standards.

Library of Congress Name Authority File (LCNAF)

The Library of Congress Name Authority File (LCNAF) is a data value standard maintained by the Library of Congress. Libraries that are members of the Program for Cooperative Cataloging Name Authority Cooperative (NACO) contribute to it, and submissions are described according to a set of standards mandated by the Library of Congress. More than eight million name authority files currently exist for people, events, corporate bodies, places, and titles, and more are added monthly.[66]

---

66 "Library of Congress Names—LC Linked Data Service (Library of Congress)," accessed August 18, 2012, http://id.loc.gov/authorities/names.html.

These bibliographic authority records include both authoritative and alternate versions of names and may include dates of existence or operation. Archivists may employ these authority records in description to distinguish between different people or organizations with the same name and to refer to the same entity consistently.

While LCNAF was originally developed for bibliographic use, the standard has been widely adopted for describing archival materials, and structure and content standards (like EAD and DACS) reference LCNAF as a source for creating access points, or the digital equivalent of entry headings in a catalog record.[67] The EAD element <persname> may be used with a SOURCE attribute to indicate the vocabulary from which the content was drawn:

```
<controlaccess>
    <persname source="lcnaf">Kennedy, John F. (John
    Fitzgerald), 1917-1963</persname>
</controlaccess>
```

Despite the number of authority records, not all creators or subjects of archival collections may be found in the LC database. Because the authority records are submitted primarily by bibliographic catalogers, the subjects of these authority records are derived from published materials rather than archival collections, which frequently contain unpublished material (and have different creators and subjects). Archivists may consult DACS (element 2.6 and Chapter 9), AACR2, or the forthcoming RDA for rules on how to form names that are not in LCNAF.

Union List of Artists' Names (ULAN)

There are also several profession-based thesauri of data value standards. One of these is the Union List of Artists' Names (ULAN), which is a standard for names of individuals or corporate bodies associated with the creation, collection, and storage of and access to visual art and architecture.[68] Created in 1984, ULAN is maintained by the Getty Research Institute, which also maintains the Art and Architecture Thesaurus (described below), the Thesaurus of Geographic Names, and the Cultural Objects Name Authority (CONA), which is still under development.

---

67 *Describing Archives: A Content Standard,* xviii.
68 Although titled a "union list," ULAN is in fact a thesaurus containing structured information. "About the ULAN (Getty Research Institution)," accessed August 19, 2012, at http://www.getty.edu/research/tools/vocabularies/ulan/about.html.

The minimum content items required for a valid name standard within ULAN are a numeric ID, a name, a role, nationality, and life dates, with the preferred form of the name indicated in each name standard. Preferred forms of names generally accord with LCNAF. Other optional information provided includes alternate names, married names, and relationships with other individuals and corporate bodies within the thesaurus. These content items map to EAC-CPF data elements. Like NACO, the Getty collects contributions to its thesaurus from other organizations.[69]

Library of Congress Subject Headings (LCSH)

The Library of Congress Subject Headings (LCSH) standard is a second data value standard maintained by the Library of Congress. LCSH is a controlled vocabulary of terms that describe the topics of bibliographic and archival materials. The Library has published the vocabulary annually since 1909; currently, it is accessible both online and in print.[70]

Subject headings may include topical terms (such as "Boats and boating"), geographic names (such as the "Monongahela River [W. Va. and Pa.]"), and genre or form headings (such as "Photographs").[71] These terms may have subheadings that further specify the subjects in terms of geography ("Forest reserves—Tennessee"), dates ("Art, Austrian—20th century"), or additional subjects ("Islamic civilization—study and teaching"). Rules govern when and how subjects may be assigned subheadings; those rules are collected in the *Classification and Shelflisting Manual*.[72]

As with LCNAF, LCSH can be access points within an EAD finding aid. In EAD, "[u]se of controlled vocabulary forms is recommended to facilitate access to the subjects within and across finding aid systems."[73] Using the same set of access points for archival materials that are used for books integrates subject access of archival materials with other

---

69 Ibid.
70 The online version is updated Monday–Saturday evenings. Library of Congress Authorities, "Help Pages," accessed August 19, 2012, http://authorities.loc.gov/help/auth-faq.htm#3. The database of terms may be found online at http://id.loc.gov/authorities/subjects.html.
71 The Getty Research Institute maintains separate thesauri for genre/form terms and geographic names. Search the Getty Thesaurus of Geographic Names at http://www.getty.edu/vow/TGNSearchPage.jsp.
72 Richard P. Smiraglia, "Subject Access to Archival Materials Using LCSH," *Cataloging and Classification Quarterly* 11, no. 3/4 (1990): 81–82. See also *Classification and Shelflisting Manual* (Washington, DC: Library of Congress, 2008), http://www.loc.gov/cds/products/product.php?productID=16 or available through the Cataloger's Desktop.
73 "<subject> Subject," Encoded Archival Description Tag Library—Version 2002, accessed August 20, 2012, http://www.loc.gov/ead/tglib/elements/subject.html.

sources in a catalog or OPAC. The EAD element <subject> may be used with a SOURCE attribute to indicate the vocabulary from which the content was drawn. In the first element described above, it might look something like this:

```
<controlaccess>
    <subject source="lcsh">Boats and boating.</subject>
</controlaccess>
```

Art and Architecture Thesaurus (AAT)

Data value standards may also describe the genre or form of a particular archival object or collection. The Art and Architecture Thesaurus (AAT), maintained by the Getty Research Institute, is a list of genre/form terms organized around concepts. Begun in the 1970s, this thesaurus represents the culmination of efforts to provide a controlled vocabulary for generic concepts relating to the description of art, architecture, and material culture to be used in automating cataloging. The thesaurus is edited and republished monthly to respond to the needs of current practice and scholarship.

The minimum description required for a valid concept in the AAT involves a numeric ID, a preferred term, and its place in the thesaurus hierarchy. Descriptive notes and non-preferred titles may also be included. AAT-preferred terms often coincide with LCSH terms. The AAT also adheres to standards of "thesaurus construction." That means, in part, that the AAT has a faceted, hierarchical arrangement that proceeds from an abstract to a concrete level.[74] For example, the entry for "correspondence" looks like this:

Objects Facet
.... Visual and Verbal Communication (Hierarchy Name) (G)
.... Information Forms (Hierarchy Name) (G)
.... <information forms (Guide Term)> (G)
.... <document genres> (G)
.... <document genres by function> (G)
.... correspondence (G)[75]

---

74 Getty Research Institute, "About the AAT," accessed August 20, 2012, http://www.getty.edu/research/tools/vocabularies/aat/about.html.
75 The (G) in the hierarchy pictured above indicates that the nested terms have a genus/species relationship with each other. Getty Research Institute, "Correspondence," accessed August 19, 2012, http://www.getty.edu/vow/AATFullDisplay?find=correspondence&logic=AND&note=&subject=300026877.

Archivists can use the AAT to provide values for the specific formats of materials found in archives. For example, rule 2.3.19 in DACS states: "Where the materials being described consist solely of one or two specific forms, supply those form(s) for the nature of the archival unit."[76] A footnote related to the rule strongly encourages archives to use a standardized vocabulary when supplying the form of material. In applying this rule to a series of letters, an archivist could consult the AAT term list and find that "correspondence" is the appropriate value to insert in the title. EAD also defines the <genreform> tag for encoding the types of material found in the collection; the value for this element, as well as genre/form elements in other data structure standards, could be drawn from the AAT.

Metadata and Companion Standards

Metadata is "data associated with either an information system or an information object for purposes of description, administration, legal requirements, technical functionality, use and usage, and preservation."[77] It describes the content, context, and structure of a system or object. In the case of libraries and archives, these systems and objects are information resources.

Metadata differs from traditional library cataloging or archival description; while it includes library catalog records and archival descriptive records, it also extends beyond the traditional formats of books or records and often serves as data about digital resources, which require additional information for their care and management. Digital resources are often made directly accessible via the Internet, and in this context of unmediated access to resources, information concerning the rights of reproduction and usage must be associated with the object to inform the user of any restrictions or allowances with regard to use of the object. Technical information associated with digital records is necessary for correct rendering of the objects.[78] Additionally, digital records can be easily manipulated; to preserve their authenticity, archivists need to capture data concerning the chain of custody of the records as well as any preservation actions that have

---

76 *Describing Archives: A Content Standard*, 21.
77 Dublin Core Metadata Initiative, "DCMI Glossary," last edited 2005, accessed August 20, 2012, http://dublincore.org/documents/usageguide/glossary.shtml.
78 Marcia Lei Zeng and Jian Qin, *Metadata* (New York: Neal-Schuman Publishers, 2008), 8.

been taken to ensure their longevity. Although archivists have two highly developed and widely adopted standards—EAD and DACS—these standards only cover a portion of the information needed to manage and administer digital records.

EAD and DACS are designed for archival description, meaning that they are well suited for describing groupings of materials that are organized in a hierarchical fashion. To aid in digital resource discovery on the Internet, or to provide more granular intellectual control, repositories may choose to describe at the item level. In such cases, they may find that the more specific guidance of *companion standards*—standards used in conjunction with each other—is more appropriate to the items they are describing. For example, when cataloging individual manuscripts, repositories may choose to use DCRM(MSS): Descriptive Cataloging of Rare Materials (Manuscripts), a standard developed specifically for describing modern manuscripts.[79] DCRM(MSS) will be part of a suite of standards designed to work in conjunction with DACS, a suite that also includes standards for the description of rare graphic materials (DCRM[G]) and rare books (DCRM[B]).[80]

Descriptive Metadata

Metadata is generally divided into three different types: descriptive, structural, and administrative. This module has focused primarily on descriptive metadata, or the data needed for resource discovery and identification. Descriptive metadata standards may include structural, administrative, or technical information, but they are predominantly used to find or locate information objects. EAD outlines the hierarchical relationships between a collection and its various parts and includes elements for encoding technical and rights information, but its purpose largely remains one of enabling discovery. Two other standards commonly used, especially for the description of digital objects, are Dublin Core and MODS.

---

79 The recommended standard for medieval and Renaissance manuscripts is Gregory A. Pass, *Descriptive Cataloging of Ancient, Medieval, Renaissance, and Early Modern Manuscripts* (AMREMM) (Chicago: Association of College and Research Libraries, 2002).

80 Association of College and Research Libraries, Rare Books and Manuscripts Section, Bibliographic Standards Committee, Descriptive Cataloging of Rare Materials (Books), (DCRM[B]), 2007, accessed August 20, 2012, http://www.loc.gov/cds/PDFdownloads/dcrm/DCRM(B)_2008.pdf. DCRM(G) is still in development. More information can be found at http://www.rbms.info/committees/bibliographic_standards/dcrm/dcrmg/dcrmg.html.

Dublin Core. Dublin Core was developed to aid resource discovery on the Internet and is often used to describe digital objects at the item level. Dublin Core is commonly expressed in the Resource Description Framework (RDF), a W3C standard for data exchange on the Web, or in XML.[81] Dublin Core was originally designed by the library community but has since been more widely adopted. It is commonly used as an export or import data format in archival data management systems, and it also serves as the approved format for the Open Archives Initiative-Protocol for Metadata Harvesting (OAI-PMH), a standard for metadata exchange between repositories.[82] Perhaps the main reason for Dublin Core's widespread use stems from its simple design: it comprises only fifteen broad and generic data elements. These simple elements proved inadequate for those interested in more detailed description. Dublin Core can be extended to include additional elements, often referred to as Qualified Dublin Core but formally known as the DCMI Metadata Terms. These terms include many additional descriptive properties, such as *audience* and *bibliographicCitation*.[83] Dublin Core has also been adapted to better describe particular types of materials. For example, PBCore is a metadata schema based on Dublin Core but extended for richer description of media materials. PBCore is commonly used in the public broadcasting community.[84]

Metadata Object Description Schema (MODS). MODS is another standard commonly used to describe digital objects. It was designed to bridge the complexity of MARC with the interoperability of Dublin Core. MODS is a part of the MARC family—its set of data elements is a subset of the MARC data element set, and those elements inherit the semantics outlined in MARC. Expressed in XML, it uses language-based tags (instead of the numeric tags employed by MARCXML), employs attributes to refine elements, and allows for hierarchical relationships between elements. MODS is an attractive standard for libraries and repositories that want to provide rich description and maintain interoperability. MODS also has a companion standard for authority records: the Metadata Authority Description Schema, or MADS.

---

81 W3C Semantic Web, "Resource Description Framework (RDF)," 2004, accessed August 20, 2012, http://www.w3.org/RDF/.
82 See the Open Archives Initiative at http://www.openarchives.org/pmh for more information.
83 See the Dublin Core Metadata Initiative at http://dublincore.org/documents/dcmi-terms/ for more information.
84 Corporation for Public Broadcasting, "About PBCore," accessed August 20, 2012, http://pbcore.org/about/.

Structural Metadata

In the digital realm, one resource may comprise several different computer files. A simple website consists of several different Web pages, as well as any images or multimedia files that may be embedded in them. A multi-page report that has been digitized may be made from the scanned images of individual pages. Digital objects composed of more than one file or depending on another file for proper rendering are known as *compound digital objects*. Structural metadata provides information on how these types of objects are put together so they can be used and displayed.

Metadata Encoding and Transmission Standard (METS). The Metadata Encoding and Transmission Standard, or METS, is an XML encoding standard for structural data maintained by the Library of Congress. METS captures the information necessary to render complex digital objects and the relationships between the files that make up that object. In addition to encoding structural data, METS also leverages the extensibility of XML by allowing for the incorporation of other standards for description and administrative metadata within a single METS record. For example, the Descriptive Metadata section, or <dmdSec>, of a METS record may contain an encoded MODS record or a Dublin Core record. Likewise, the Administrative Metadata, or <amdSec>, section of the same record may contain encoded PREMIS data (see below). METS contains several other sections that define the structure of the object:

- The File Section, or <fileSec>, lists all the files that the digital object comprises. These files <file> can be grouped using the <fileGrp> to list the different versions of an object. For example, thumbnails of the individual files may be grouped in one <fileGrp>, while the master versions are listed in another <fileGrp>.
- The Structural Map, or <structMap>, points to the files listed in the <fileSec> and delineates the hierarchy and order of the files.
- The Structural Links, or <structLink>, section is used to record the existence of hyperlinks between items within the Structural Map, which is useful for describing relationships within a website.
- The Behavioral Section, or <behaviorSec>, can be used to associate executable behaviors with METS content.[85]

---

85 Library of Congress, "METS: An Overview & Tutorial," 2011, accessed August 20, 2012, http://www.loc.gov/standards/mets/METSOverview.v2.html.

Administrative Metadata

Administrative metadata captures information useful for resource management and includes technical information, preservation metadata, and rights management information.

PREservation Metadata: Implementation Strategies (PREMIS). Especially important in managing digital resources over the long term, preservation metadata captures a variety of essential information, including:

- the provenance and custodial history of the digital resource;
- checksums, which can ensure a file's integrity and authenticity;
- authorized preservation actions undertaken by the repository to ensure a resource's longevity, such as normalization or migration;
- information concerning what software is needed to render the digital resource; and
- the type and age of the storage medium.

PREMIS is the most commonly used preservation metadata standard. It captures information necessary to ensure an object's long-term access as well as its authenticity. PREMIS consists of a data model and a data dictionary. The PREMIS data model contains five interacting entities: Intellectual Entity, Object, Event, Rights, and Agents. The PREMIS data dictionary outlines the semantic units needed to describe the entities in order to carry out digital preservation functions. PREMIS can be expressed in XML or in RDF. PREMIS is extensible—other schemas can be used to extend the information captured in a PREMIS record, such as Metadata for Images in XML (MIX), a schema often used for capturing technical metadata for digital images, such as color space and compression type. PREMIS is frequently used within METS records; in fact, its elements can be implemented within the administrative metadata section of a METS record.[86]

The Semantic Web and Linked Data

The development of the Social Networks and Archival Contexts (SNAC) project (discussed below), the revision of EAD, and the continuing revisions of many of the metadata standards outlined

---

86 For more information on using PREMIS with METS, see http://www.loc.gov/standards/premis/premis-mets.html.

Standards for Archival Description 53

above all reflect an awareness and integration of Semantic Web and Linked Data technologies into archival descriptive standards and practice. The World Wide Web has historically consisted of documents: information resources with a Uniform Resource Identifier (URI) that returns representations—for example, HTML Web pages or JPG images—of the resource in response to Hypertext Transfer Protocol (HTTP) requests.[87] The Semantic Web is a web of data, or, more specifically, Linked Data. On the Semantic Web, URIs identify not just documents, but real-world objects such as people, places, and things, as well as intangible things, like ideas. Semantic Web and Linked Data technologies define and describe these objects and things in a manner that is machine-actionable, thus providing the language for defining "how data relates to real-world objects."[88] For example, take the statement:

John F. Kennedy wrote Profiles in Courage.

The sentence can be broken down into three parts: the subject (John F. Kennedy), the predicate (authored), and the object (the book titled *Profiles in Courage*). We can use the URIs to represent all three parts of the statement, in a form that information scientists call a *triple*.

Profiles in Courage: http://www.worldcat.org/title/profiles-in
-courage/oclc/420704
The concept of creating: http://purl.org/dc/terms/creator
John F. Kennedy: http://id.loc.gov/authorities/names/n79055297

Using RDF expressed in XML (RDF/XML), that statement may look something like Figure 5.

By using the same language to define things, their attributes, and their relationships to one another, archivists can connect data to other data in ways previously not possible. Linked Data is attractive to libraries and archives for just that reason; data once trapped in a silo—for example, an online library catalog—can now be connected

---

87 W3C Interest Group, "Cool URIs for the Semantic Web," last updated 2008, accessed August 20, 2012, http://www.w3.org/TR/cooluris/#oldweb.
88 W3C, "W3C Semantic Web Activity," 2012, accessed August 20, 2012, http://www.w3.org/2001/sw/.

> **Figure 5. RDF/XML Example**
>
> ```
> <?xml version="1.0"?>
> <rdf:RDF
> xmlns:rdf="http://www.w3.org/1999/02/22-rdf-syntax-ns#"
> xmlns:dc= "http://purl.org/dc/elements/1.1/">
> ```
>
> (calls both the RDF and Dublin Core namespaces, which define the elements used below)
>
> ```
>   <rdf:Description rdf:about="http://www.worldcat.org/
>   title/profiles-in-courage/oclc/420704">
> ```
>
> (RDF statement that the following description is about the book *Profiles in Courage*.)
>
> ```
>     <dc:creator(Dublin Core statment for creator)>
>     http://id.loc.gov/authorities/names/n79055297
> ```
>
> (URL for John F. Kennedy)
>
> ```
>     </dc:creator>
>   </rdf:Description>
> </rdf:RDF>
> ```

to data from other sources.[89] Content can be rediscovered, reused, and remixed. The Semantic Web introduces a whole new suite of standards: SKOS, RDF, OWL, SPARQL, and others. By repurposing archival description using these standards, archivists can not only share their data with an audience that is much larger than ever before, but they can also incorporate description-enhancing, context-laden data from other sources. A full explanation of Semantic Web and Linked Data concepts and technologies is beyond the scope of this module. See the Further Reading section for resources that provide more detailed information.

Archival Standards in Action

EAD Consortia

As mentioned previously, one major benefit of standardizing archival description is to bring multiple finding aids together in one place,

---

[89] For additional information, see Diane M. Zorich, Gunter Waibel, and Ricky Erway, *Beyond the Silos of the LAMs: Collaboration Among Libraries, Archives and Museums* (Dublin, OH: OCLC Research, 2009), accessed August 19, 2012, http://www.oclc.org/resources/research/publications/library/2008/2008-05.pdf.

Standards for Archival Description   55

enabling researchers to search a single system, rather than multiple repositories, for relevant materials. This is realized most fully in the finding aids consortia that have developed with the adoption of EAD. These consortia tend to organize around geography, such as the Online Archive of California (OAC). Developed by University of California institutions, it now hosts more than twenty thousand EAD finding aids from more than two hundred California-based libraries, historical societies, museums, and special collections. Other notable EAD consortia include the Northwest Digital Archives (NWDA) and Texas Archival Resources Online (TARO).

The Social Networks and Archival Context Project (SNAC)

The advent of EAC-CPF has enabled the creation of a catalog of archival authority records that not only provides biographical information on a person, family, or corporate body and variant forms of name, but also links the person to related archival materials and to other persons, families, or corporate bodies. SNAC is a collaborative project between the University of Virginia; University of California, Berkeley; and the California Digital Library. Data for the project is being provided by the Library of Congress, the OAC, NWDA, Virginia Heritage, and others. SNAC's objective is to derive EAC-CPF records from existing EAD records; match those names to other EAD records as well as name records in authority files like LCNAF, ULAN, and the Virtual International Authority File (VIAF); winnow out duplicate names; and match name variants with each other.

The SNAC prototype system allows users a means to browse and search creator names and their related archival materials, providing graphic visualizations of relationships between creators.[90] Visualizations of the creators' social networks can aid researchers in identifying additional material relevant to their searches. By making relationships apparent, researchers are given a broader, more detailed context in which they can identify who was corresponding with whom, allowing them to explore how creators influenced each other. As part of the second phase of SNAC, which is supported by the Andrew W. Mellon Foundation, records from thirteen state and regional

---

90 SNAC: Social Networks and Archival Context Project, "Prototype," accessed August 20, 2012, http://socialarchive.iath.virginia.edu/prototype.html.

archival consortia and thirty-five university and national repositories, including the National Archives and Records Administration (NARA) and the British Library, will be included in the system. Two million bibliographic records from OCLC will also be added.[91]

Archival Data Management Software

EAD and other XML files can be time-consuming to create by hand. Repositories have devised several means of making this process more efficient, such as developing templates, which contain boilerplate text for repetitive fields, and finding ways to automate the markup process. In the past five years, several data management systems designed specifically for archival data have been introduced to the field.

These systems were designed to be standards-compliant and produce standard output, such as EAD, METS, or MARCXML. They also capture accessioning information and other administrative information related to managing and describing archival collections. The two systems most widely used in the United States are the Archivists' Toolkit and Archon.[92] ICA-AtoM, a product supported by the ICA, is widely adopted internationally. All three programs are available as open-source software. There are also a number of proprietary software programs available, such as Cuadra STAR and Eloquent Archives.[93]

In addition to managing archival data and producing EAD and other standard output, there also exists the need to display that data online in a meaningful and searchable manner.[94] The OAC and several other archival institutions use the eXtensible Text Framework (XTF) system, which can index and search XML data and display it via XSLT. Omeka, a website content management system designed for digital humanities projects, has become increasingly popular in the last few

---

91 Jennifer Howard, "Project Aims to Build Online Hub for Archival Materials," *Chronicle of Higher Education*, May 13, 2012, accessed August 20, 2012, http://chronicle.com/article/Building-a-Digital-Map-of/131846/.
92 A new system, ArchivesSpace, is currently under development and is slated to replace the Archivists' Toolkit and Archon. See http://www.archivesspace.org/.
93 For more information, see Lisa Spiro, *Archival Management Software: A Report for the Council on Library and Information Resources* (Washington, DC: CLIR, 2009), accessed August 20, 2012, http://www.clir.org/pubs/reports/spiro/spiro2009.html/spiro/spiro_Jan13.pdf.
94 Most modern browsers can read and display XML. Repositories with limited technical resources may choose to place XML finding aids directly online with a style sheet to control the display of the XML elements, and they can add a box that offers users a Google site search as well.

years and offers a quick and fairly easy way of placing not only finding aid information but also digital resources online.[95] Additionally, several traditional Integrated Library Systems (ILS) vendors have begun offering ways of integrating EAD-encoded finding aids and other XML-encoded standards into the traditional online catalog. Some of the same systems available for EAD authoring—Archon and ICA-AtoM—also display finding aids online. For more information on archival systems, please see Module 3, *Designing Descriptive and Access Systems* by Daniel A. Santamaria in Trends in Archives Practice.

Standards Revisions

Standards are not static. Descriptive needs may change in response to external issues, such as new legislation, or the development of new information formats, like animated gifs, which require additional types of description or new controlled vocabulary terms. Standards must be maintained and updated to ensure their continued usefulness. The SAA Standards Committee has slated a review period of five years for each of the standards it espouses. Currently, both EAD and DACS are undergoing review.

EAD was last revised in 2002, and technology, especially Internet technology, has changed much since then. Although the revision is still very much in development, one of the points of emphasis for the EAD revision is to achieve greater conceptual and semantic consistency in its use.[96] Because the standard was designed to handle the main archival descriptive tool of the time—the finding aid—it takes on the document-centric characteristics of that tool. It provides the model for a document that describes archival collections but does not formally model archival collections and their complex components as entities themselves.[97] Generally, the proposed revisions seek to (1) increase consistency by eliminating the possibility of encoding the same information in multiple ways; (2) exchange or incorporate data

---

95   EAD-encoded finding aids can be placed in Omeka using a plug-in offered on the Omeka site that transforms finding aids into Dublin Core; this functionality is not part of the core software.
96   Society of American Archivists, Technical Subcommittee for Encoded Archival Description, "EAD Revision: Points of Emphasis," February 22, 2012, accessed August 20, 2012, http://www2.archivists.org/sites/all/files/EAD%20Revision-Points%20of%20 Emphasis.pdf.
97   TS-EAD, "EAD-Technical Considerations," accessed August 20, 2012, http://www2 .archivists.org/sites/all/files/EADRevisionTechnicalConsiderations.pdf.

maintained under other protocols; and (3) improve the use of EAD in international or multilingual environments.[98]

DACS is also currently undergoing revision. It was originally written when EAD was the main structure standard for archival description. The introduction of EAC-CPF has resulted in the need for a revision of the DACS elements that contain contextual information as part of collection description. More specific changes are discussed throughout the above section on DACS.

In addition to the revision of EAD and DACS, the library content standard AACR2 is being replaced by RDA, a new standard based on the Functional Requirements for Bibliographic Records (FRBR) model.[99] This model focuses on entities and relationships and is strikingly different than the traditional ISBD model.

Archival Description for Your Repository: Choosing the Right Standards

This module has outlined a variety of standards, each of which was designed to accomplish different purposes. So how do you choose the standards that are right for your repository?

As Jody DeRidder writes, "Intelligent selection requires careful assessment of internal needs and resources, as well as careful assessment of the options. If user and client needs are not weighed, the outcome will be a tremendous disappointment."[100] While this statement refers to choosing software for a digital library, it is also good advice for choosing descriptive standards. The questions and ideas listed below (concerning institutional factors, the nature of the materials being described, and community context) are intended to help you select the standards that work best for your institution, your community and your materials. Daniel A. Santamaria's module in this series (Module 3) also provides good advice regarding software packages that support archival description, focusing on specific tools and services that can support descriptive work.

---

98   Society of American Archivists, "EAD Revision."
99   The Library of Congress plans to adopt RDA as a descriptive standard. More information about the time line for that process may be accessed at http://www.loc.gov /aba/rda/index.html.
100 Jody L. DeRidder, "Choosing Software for a Digital Library," *Library Hi Tech News* 9, no. 10 (2007): 19.

Standards for Archival Description 59

Institutional Factors

Your choice of standards depends on your institution's needs and resources. Selecting a standard requires you to consider future possibilities (How might we wish to share data in five years?) while balancing the constraints of the present (A frozen salary line means that most encoding work will be done by current or volunteer staff).

Before implementing a new descriptive practice, you should conduct a survey of your existing description practices and resources; you should also assess expected end-user needs.

Descriptive Practice

- What kind of description do you already have, and in what formats does it exist (examples: finding aids, collection summaries, catalog records)? Can this description easily be converted into a standardized format, and if so, using which descriptive standards?
- Does the description already adhere to any standards, including older versions of an existing standard? If not, is the description consistent? For example, while you may not refer to people according to LCNAF, you may refer to them using internal consistency in each descriptive record.
- To what level are your collections described? Do you have items that have been described/cataloged individually?
- How portable, or shareable, is this descriptive information? Is it only available as a paper document copy? Is it on a computer, but in a proprietary or uncommon program or system? Is the information structured, as in a spreadsheet or database, or is it in free text form? Is it in an older or outdated version of a common program?
- Is your institution using any systems that require the use of particular standards?
- Do you receive collections with donor- or creator-supplied description? If so, what standards (if any) do they adhere to, and what file format do they use for description?

60 ARCHIVAL ARRANGEMENT AND DESCRIPTION

Description Resources

- Who on your staff describes archival materials? Do you have trained archivists or librarians? What volunteers, paraprofessionals, or student employees do you have at your disposal? How are these staff trained, and what kind of resources do you have available for training? Most standards require a few minimum fields; even if you choose a standard that allows for the encapsulation of rich metadata, you may decide to ignore many of the optional elements because you do not have staffing support.
- What hardware and software constraints do you face? How much technical support will adoption of a certain standard require? Will you need to purchase software or implement a new system to support the standard?
- If you work in a repository that is part of a larger institution, does that institution hold library or archival materials? What resources has the larger institution put toward description that you could use?
- Do you currently contribute descriptive information (catalog records, EAD finding aids) to any shared catalogs or consortia? If so, how do their practices influence your description? What impact would a change in procedure have on your contributions to consortia or shared catalogs?
- Are you currently engaged in collaborative data-sharing projects with other organizations or institutions? If so, does the project require certain descriptive practices? Could those descriptive practices be extended to other collections or items?
- If your repository has electronic records or digitized records, do those records require specialized practices?
- What type of description (metadata or other) does your IT department support or require?
- If you have received or are considering applying for grant funding, do the terms of the grant require you to adopt certain descriptive standards? For example, National Historical Publication and Records Commission (NHPRC) Documenting Democracy: Access to Historical Records Projects require grant recipients to produce either MARC records (to be entered in a national catalog) or EAD-compliant finding aids (to be

submitted to regional or national consortia).¹⁰¹ Participation in the Council on Library and Information Resources (CLIR) Hidden Collections Program "requires the application of standards for processing and description that would provide interoperability and long-term sustainability for project data in the online environment."¹⁰²

User Needs

How do users find your materials? If your repository routinely conducts reference interviews, it may be helpful to ask how users found your materials and/or your institution. You may discover that the bulk of your users are finding your collections through Internet searches rather than through your library catalog, which could influence you to allocate more resources toward publishing and displaying finding aids online.

When you have a sense of your current descriptive practice and how it is used, consider what additional standards you would like to adopt. These standards may be suggested by the nature of your collections or by the practices of your professional or geographic community.

Nature of the Materials

Perhaps the most important consideration when choosing descriptive standards is the nature of the records or manuscripts being described. Guidelines for descriptive metadata disseminated by the Research Libraries Group (RLG) suggest that you should "determine the most appropriate descriptive approach and standard for the materials. This process of materials analysis considers how the materials are to be grouped and organized, and what aspects are to be described, how, and for what purposes.... [T]his analysis also investigates which data content rules, thesauri, or name authorities may be appropriate for the materials, and for which fields authority control has to be established."¹⁰³

---

101 National Historical Publications and Records Commission, "Documenting Democracy: Access to Historic Records Projects," accessed August 19, 2012, http://www.archives.gov/nhprc/announcement/access.html.
102 Council on Library and Information Resources, "About the Hidden Collections Program," accessed August 19, 2012, http://www.clir.org/hiddencollections.
103 *Descriptive Metadata Guidelines for RLG Cultural Materials* (Mountain View, CA: Research Libraries Group: 2005), 7, accessed October 11, 2012, http://www.oclc.org/research/activities/past/rlg/culturalmaterials/RLG_desc_metadata.pdf.

As you survey your collections, consider the following:

- Are your materials mainly archival, bibliographic, electronic, or a mix of different formats? If your holdings are varied, you may wish to adopt standards that can be used across all formats. Data value standards, such as LCNAF and LCSH, and structure standards, such as EAD, could be used for all three types of collections, with specific metadata and companion standards being used depending on the format (for example, PREMIS and METS for electronic materials or DCRM[B] for rare books).
- What genres of material or file types are contained in your collections? Some standards are designed specifically to account for the different information needs associated with particular formats and types of materials. As mentioned above, PBCore was developed to describe audiovisual media; if such media do not appear in your holdings, adopting PBCore will be unnecessary. In the same way, technical metadata like MIX applies only to photographs and not to other digital resources, such as e-mail. Additionally, not all standards are optimal for recording all types of information.
- What level of description is warranted? DACS and EAD are designed for multi-level hierarchical description (although both can be used for collection-level description). Other standards excel at providing description at the item level.
- What type of description is necessary based on the format of the materials and how the materials will be accessed? For example, collecting and sharing rights information is more important for digital materials shared online with unmediated access. You may choose not to collect or maintain administrative metadata about other collections for which access will be mediated.

Community Context

Participating in a consortium or contributing records to NACO or the Getty Vocabulary Program[104] increases exposure to your collections and, more generally, adds to discoverable knowledge. Most organi-

---

104 The Getty Vocabulary Program has its own XML schema for contributions, although online submission of content through a webform is also possible. The Getty Research Institute, "Contribute to Getty Vocabularies," accessed August 19, 2012, http://www.getty.edu/research/tools/vocabularies/contribute.html.

zations require that your submissions adhere to certain descriptive standards and even particular ways of adhering to these standards; for example, EAD consortia often request that submissions be encoded in specific ways.[105] Consider what organizations you belong to, or wish to join, and how compliance with their required description would affect your descriptive practice. Conversely, consider how maintaining your description according to less-common standards would affect your ability to share descriptive data with other institutions or organizations or to publish that description on the Web.

You may also want to consider more broadly the communities in which you exist. What standards are used by other repositories with similar resources and collections or at peer institutions?[106] Which standards are approved by the professional organization(s) to which you belong? Investigating which standards are espoused by your professional organization, and what standards are used by similar organizations, will give you an idea of which ones you should consider.

Conclusion

When we describe archives, we provide information about a collection's context, content, structure, and functions. Descriptive standards not only help us capture this information in a consistent manner, but they also make it easier to index and display information. Implementing descriptive standards is neither a simple nor an easy process, but by doing so, you will reap benefits for you and for your collections. Best of all, you will also make it easier for people to find, understand, and use the records and manuscripts under your care.

Adopting standards will help you.

Description of the materials in our holdings lies at the core of what we do as archivists. Adopting descriptive standards will only change

---

105 See, for example, the Online Archive of California's standards for EAD submission to that consortium. OAC Working Group, Metadata Standards Subcommittee, "OAC Best Practice Guidelines for EAD," accessed August 19, 2012, http://www.cdlib.org/services/dsc/contribute/docs/oacbpgead_v2-0.pdf.

106 For a 2008 survey of metadata creation/maintenance practices at RLG institutions, see Leighann Ayers et al., *What We've Learned from the RLG Partners Metadata Creation Workflows Survey* (Dublin, OH: OCLC Research, 2009), accessed October 11, 2012, http://www.oclc.org/resources/research/publications/library/2009/2009-04.pdf.

how you carry out this function. Standardized description will also help you manage your collections: consistent description provides you with a better sense of the extent and nature of your holdings. Adopting archival descriptive standards affirms your participation in your professional community.

Adopting standards will help your description.

Good archival description goes beyond the *what* of the resources in our care. It communicates the context of these resources, *how* they came to be and *who* helped create them. Adhering to standards can also make your role in description more transparent, communicating to users how and why your description includes certain elements or content. Changing your descriptive practice to incorporate standards will take time and require that decisions be made about how to allocate often-scarce resources. But it will also result in richer and more useful information about your collections.

Adopting standards will help your descriptions get discovered.

Adhering to data content and value standards prepares a repository to adopt data structure standards in the future. Moving into an electronic environment—that is, migrating, mapping, and marking up your description—becomes infinitely less complicated if description is standardized from the beginning. Once archival descriptions are held in a standardized format, it is much easier to incorporate them into access technologies, making it much easier for the end users of archives to discover and use the records.

Standardizing data and using descriptive standards will only become more important over time. For example, we can take advantage of new advances to repurpose data that was developed or stored according to the recommendations of archival standards. We can also adopt standards developed outside our profession, in order to increase the visibility of our collections and to disseminate them to new audiences.

Technologies and user search patterns change rapidly, and adhering to standardized description means that your collections will be discovered in new environments. As Jennifer Schaffner of OCLC notes, "Invisibility of archives, manuscripts and special collections may well have more to do with the metadata we create than with the interfaces we build. Now that we no longer control discovery, the metadata that we contribute is critical. In so many ways, the metadata *is* the interface."[107]

---

[107] Jennifer Schaffner, *The Metadata Is the Interface: Better Description for Better Discovery of Archives and Special Collections* (Dublin, OH: OCLC Programs and Research, 2009), 4, accessed October 11, 2012, http://www.oclc.org/research/publications/library/2009/2009-06.pdf.

Appendix A: Case Studies

Summary of the UCSD DAMS System

by Bradley Westbrook

Library staff have developed and refined a workflow for building and ingesting digital objects into the University of California, San Diego Libraries Digital Asset Management System (DAMS). The workflow begins with the approval of a digital library project. Once approved, staff prepares content files and metadata, including rights assessments, for ingest.

Ingest follows two pathways. In one pathway, content files are transferred to the DAMS and assigned archival resource keys (ARKs), a type of persistent identifier. Technical metadata is extracted using JHOVE and other extractors, and a partial object record is registered in the DAMS. In the other pathway, metadata analysts normalize source descriptive metadata, which is typically received as an Excel file or as database output, MARC records, or Archivists' Toolkit exports. An object specification is created for a given project, with a set of rules for transforming and enriching the source metadata to satisfy the requirements of both the project and the DAMS. Metadata formats supported by the DAMS include MODS for description, PREMIS for files and rights, and MIX for additional information about still image content.

With the object specification in hand, library programmers build the individual objects constituting a project, using XSLT and other transformation methods to convert all metadata to RDF statements and to join the partial record, the additional metadata, and the structural metadata into a single, integrated object record. The workflow for a project concludes with the registration of the completed objects into the triplestore holding the DAMS data (https://libraries.ucsd.edu/digital/). A slightly more technical overview of the workflow is available at http://tpot.ucsd.edu/metadata-services/mas/data-workflow.html.

What We Learned at ECU by Experimenting with EAC
by Mark Custer

East Carolina University's Joyner Library outsourced the encoding of their finding aids in 2001–2002 with the assistance of an NC ECHO LSTA[108] legacy finding aid grant. The result: just over 1,000 manuscript collections were encoded in EAD. Once in EAD, the collections were ready for the Web, but they were still waiting for EAC-CPF to help expose and untangle the richly interconnected web that was woven throughout their archival descriptions.

Fast-forward to 2011, and the number of EAD records managed by Joyner Library had increased to 1,846. At this time, the EAC-CPF standard had been officially released, and the Social Networks and Archival Context project (SNAC) had created an online EAC-driven prototype. Still, the majority of names in ECU's collections were not yet represented in the SNAC database. The stage was set, then, to experiment with creating our very own EAC-CPF records. What we learned in the process was invaluable.

Contained within our 1,846 EAD records were more than 6,000 encoded names (80 percent personal names) and 716 biographical or historical notes. Terry Sanford, for example, appeared in thirteen of the collections, with the following type of encoding being typical:

```
<persname> Sanford, Terry (7) 1958, 1961</persname>
```

Not only could we leverage this data to authorize the names, but we were able to "link" many of them with external services, such as OCLC's Virtual International Authority File (VIAF), with the help of Google Refine, as shown on the next page:

---

108 For additional information on the North Carolina Exploring Cultural Heritage Online (ECHO) Project, see http://www.ncecho.org/grants/index.shtml. For more information on Library Services and Technology Act (LSTA) Grants, see http://statelibrary.ncdcr.gov/ld/grants/lsta.html.

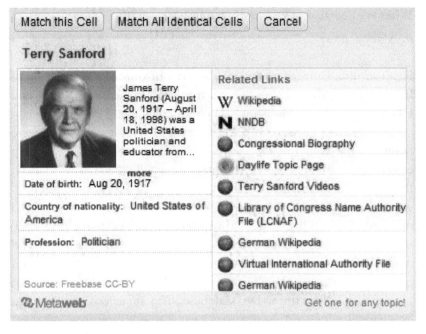

EAC-CPF Authority Data in OCLC VAIF

All told, the experiment resulted in 3,415 unique names. But its value will really shine through once these EAC-CPF records are shared and controlled by the entire archival community.

Appendix B: Further Reading

Guidance on Standards

Ayers, Leighann, et al. *What We've Learned from the RLG Partners Metadata Creation Workflows Survey*. Dublin, OH: OCLC Research, 2009. http://www.oclc.org/resources/research/publications/library/2009/2009-04.pdf.

Descriptive Metadata Guidelines for RLG Cultural Materials. Mountain View, CA: Research Libraries Group, 2005. http://www.oclc.org/research/activities/past/rlg/culturalmaterials/RLG_desc_metadata.pdf. See especially Appendix A for recommendations on what standards to use for what purposes.

Digital Library Federation Aquifer Public Metadata Documents, https://wiki.dlib.indiana.edu/display/DLFAquifer/DLF+Aquifer+Public+Metadata+Documents. Includes the Digital Library Federation/Aquifer Implementation Guidelines for Shareable Metadata and other guidelines for implementing MODS.

MacNeil, Heather. "Trusting Description: Authenticity, Accountability, and Archival Description Standards." *Journal of Archival Organization* 7, no. 3 (2009): 89–107.

Society of American Archivists Standards Portal. http://www2.archivists.org/standards.

Standards

AACR2

Gorman, Michael. *The Concise AACR*. Chicago: American Library Association, 2004.

DACS

Society of American Archivists. *Describing Archives: A Content Standard.* Chicago: Society of American Archivists, 2004.

Dublin Core

Dublin Core Metadata Initiative. http://dublincore.org.

EAC-CPF

Encoded Archival Context—Corporate Bodies, Persons, and Families. http://eac.staatsbibliothek-berlin.de/.

SNAC: The Social Networks and Archival Context Project. http://socialarchive.iath.virginia.edu/prototype.html.

EAC-CPF Tag Library. http://www3.iath.virginia.edu/eac/cpf/tagLibrary/cpfTagLibrary.html.

EAD

Encoded Archival Description—Version 2002. http://www.loc.gov/ead.

Dow, Elizabeth H. "Encoded Archival Description as a Halfway Technology." *Journal of Archival Organization* 7, no. 3 (2009): 108–115.

SAA EAD Roundtable. http://www2.archivists.org/groups/encoded-archival-description-ead-roundtable.

MARC

MARC Standards. http://www.loc.gov/marc.

MARC 21 Formats. http://www.loc.gov/marc/marcdocz.html

. MARCXML. http://www.loc.gov/standards/marcxml.

METS

Metadata Encoding & Transmission Standard. http://www.loc.gov/standards/mets.

MODS

Metadata Object Description Schema. http://www.loc.gov/standards/mods/.

PREMIS

Lavoie, Brian. "PREMIS with a Fresh Coat of Paint: Highlights from the Revision of the PREMIS Data Dictionary for Preservation Metadata." *D-Lib Magazine* 14, no. 5/6 (2008). http://www.dlib.org/dlib/may08/lavoie/05lavoie.html.

Preservation Metadata Maintenance Activity. http://www.loc.gov/standards/premis/.

RDA

RDA Toolkit. http://www.rdatoolkit.org/.
Joint Steering Committee for the Development of RDA. http://www.rda-jsc.org/rda.html.

More on Metadata

Baca, Murtha. *Introduction to Metadata: Pathways to Digital Information*. Los Angeles: Getty Information Institute, 1998.
Riley, Jenn. *Glossary of Metadata Standards*. http://dlib.indiana.edu/~jenlrile/metadatamap/seeingstandards_glossary_pamphlet.pdf.
Riley, Jenn, and Kelcy Shepherd. "A Brave New World: Archivists and Shareable Descriptive Metadata." *American Archivist* 72 (Spring/Summer 2009): 91–112.
Schaffner, Jennifer. *The Metadata Is the Interface: Better Description for Better Discovery of Archives and Special Collections*. Dublin, OH: OCLC Programs and Research, 2009. http://www.oclc.org/research/publications/library/2009/2009-06.pdf.
Smith-Yoshimura, Karen. *RLG Programs Descriptive Metadata Practices Survey Results*. Dublin, OH: OCLC Programs and Research, 2007. http://www.oclc.org/research/publications/library/2007/2007-03.pdf.
Zeng, Marcia Lei, and Jian Qin. *Metadata*. New York: Neal-Schuman Publishers, 2008.

ICA Standards

ISAAR(CPF). http://www.ica.org/download.php?id=1648.
ISAD(G). http://www.ica.org/download.php?id=1687.
ISDF. http://www.wien2004ica.org/sites/default/files/ISDF%20ENG.pdf.
ISDIAH. http://www.wien2004ica.org/en/node/38884.

XML

W3C specification. http://www.w3.org/XML/.
W3Schools tutorial. http://www.w3schools.com/xml/xml_whatis.asp.
O'Reilly XML resources. http://oreilly.com/xml/.

Data Value Standards

Art and Architecture Thesaurus. http://www.getty.edu/research/tools/vocabularies/aat/index.html.

Hickey, Thomas. "The Virtual International Authority File: Expanding the Concept of Universal Bibliographic Control." *NextSpace* 13 (September 2009): 18–19. http://www.oclc.org/nextspace/013/research.htm.

LC Standards, Linked Data Service, Authorities and Vocabularies. http://id.loc.gov.

The LCSH Century: One Hundred Years with the Library of Congress Subject Headings System. Special issue of *Cataloging and Classification Quarterly* 29, nos. 1–2 (2000).

Smiraglia, Richard P. "Subject Access to Archival Materials Using LCSH." *Cataloging and Classification Quarterly* 11, no. 3/4 (1990): 63–90.

Taylor, Arlene, et al., eds. *Authority Control in Organizing and Accessing Information: Definition and International Experience.* Binghamton, NY: Haworth Press, 2004.

ULAN. http://wws.getty.edu/vow/ULANSearchPage.jsp.

Semantic Web and Linked Data

Berners-Lee, Tim. TED talk. http://www.ted.com/talks/tim_berners_lee_on_the_next_web.html.

Berners-Lee, Tim, James Hendler, and Ora Lassila. "The Semantic Web." *Scientific American* 284, no. 5 (May 2001): 35–43.

Linked Data—Connect Distributed Data Across the Web. http://linkeddata.org.

Report of the Stanford Linked Data Workshop, 27 June–1 July 2011. http://www.clir.org/pubs/abstract/reports/pub152.

Voss, Jon. "An Introduction to Linked Open Data in Libraries, Archives, and Museums." September 15, 2011. http://lod-lam.net/summit/2011/09/15/intro-to-lodlam-talk-live-from-the-smithsonian/.

World Wide Web Consortium (W3C). Cool URIs for the Semantic Web. http://www.w3.org/TR/cooluris/.

———. Linked Data Rules. http://www.w3.org/DesignIssues/LinkedData.html.

_____. RDF Primer. http://www.w3.org/TR/rdf-primer.
_____. Semantic Web. http://www.w3.org/standards/semanticweb.
_____. What Is Linked Data?. http://www.w3.org/standards/semanticweb/data.

Archival Data Management Software
Archivists' Toolkit. http://www.archiviststoolkit.org.
ArchivesSpace. http://www.archivesspace.org.
Archon. http://www.archon.org.
Cuadra Star. http://www.cuadra.com/products/products.html.
Eloquent Archives. http://eloquent-systems.com/products/archives.shtml.
Spiro, Lisa. *Archival Management Software: A Report for the Council on Library and Information Resources.* January 2009. http://clir.org/pubs/reports/spiro2009.html.
Spiro, Lisa, ed. Welcome to Archival Software. http://archivalsoftware.pbworks.com/w/page/13600254/FrontPage.
XTF. http://xtf.cdlib.org.

Appendix C: Acronyms Relating to Archival Description

AACR and AACR2: Anglo-American Cataloguing Rules
First published in 1967, AACR/AACR2 are data content standards used in libraries for MARC bibliographic elements. Slated to be replaced by RDA.
Website: http://www.aacr2.org/about.html

AAT: Art and Architecture Thesaurus
Begun in the 1970s, the AAT is a data value standard that provides a controlled vocabulary for concepts relating to the description of art, architecture, and material culture. Used in bibliographic and archival environments.
Website: http://www.getty.edu/research/tools/vocabularies/aat/index.html

AMREMM: Descriptive Cataloging of Ancient, Medieval, Renaissance, and Early Modern Manuscripts
Written by Gregory Pass and published by the Association of College and Research Libraries in 2003, AMREMM serves as a supplement to AACR2 for the description of manuscripts and the creation of MARC 21 records for them.
Website: http://www.rbms.info/committees/bibliographic_standards/amremm.shtml (Note: The full standard is not available online, and a print copy must be purchased from the publisher.)

APPM: Archives, Personal Papers, and Manuscripts
Steven L. Hensen compiled APPM, published by the Library of Congress, in 1983. APPM is considered the first archival content standard and is based on AACR2. It diverges from that standard in focusing on the provenance of records, describing materials at the collection level rather than the item level and recognizing that records often were used in ways other than their creators intended.

ARK: Archival Resource Key
ARKs are URLs (or uniform resource locators) used to identify collections, items, people, organizations, objects, or ideas. They may be used as persistent identifiers in digital asset management systems.
Website: https://confluence.ucop.edu/display/Curation/ARK

CONA: Cultural Objects Name Authority
CONA is an authority list for cultural works, including works of art and buildings. The Getty maintains the list, with authority files contributed by other institutions. The search function for this vocabulary is still under development.
Website: http://www.getty.edu/research/tools/vocabularies/cona/

CSS: Cascading Stylesheets
Stylesheet languages, such as CSS, tell a browser what to make a Web document look like.
Website: http://www.w3.org/Style/CSS/Overview.en.html

DACS: Describing Archives: A Content Standard
DACS was first approved as an SAA standard for describing the content of archival collections and manuscripts in 2004. It is a U.S. standard, published in book form by SAA and based on the principles put forth in international standards ISAD(G) and ISAAR(CPF), and it replaced APPM.
Website: http://www2.archivists.org/standards/describing-archives-a-content-standard-dacs

DAMS: Digital Asset Management System
DAMS are systems that aid archivists, librarians, records managers, and anyone who manages digital files and/or digital description. They may be open source or proprietary; they may be designed specifically for archives, or they may be designed for the broader market.

DCRM(B): Descriptive Cataloging of Rare Materials (Books)
This companion standard for description of rare books was developed by the Rare Books and Manuscripts Section (RBMS) of the Association of College and Research Libraries (ACRL). The standard was last published in 2008.
Website: http://www.rbms.info/committees/bibliographic_standards/dcrm/dcrmtext.html
The full text of the standard is available online at http://www.loc.gov/cds/PDFdownloads/dcrm/DCRM(B)_2008.pdf.

DCRM(G): Descriptive Cataloging of Rare Materials (Graphics)

This companion standard for description of graphic material (from cartoons to architectural drawings) was compiled by Elisabeth Betz Parker in 1982. RBMS is currently sponsoring the development of a second version of this standard.

Website (standard still under revision): http://www.rbms.info/committees/bibliographic_standards/dcrm/dcrmg/dcrmg.html

DCRM(MSS): Descriptive Cataloging of Rare Materials (Manuscripts)

This companion standard for the description of manuscripts was developed in 2004 by RBMS to provide a standard for item-level description of manuscripts that would contain elements of archival descriptive standards, like DACS, and bibliographic descriptive standards, like ISBD.

Website (under development): http://www.rbms.info/committees/bibliographic_standards/dcrm/dcrmmss/dcrmmss.html

DCMI: Dublin Core Metadata Initiative

This organization maintains a series of standards and other specifications for description, including the descriptive metadata elements of Dublin Core.

Website: http://dublincore.org/

DTD: Document Type Definition

A DTD outlines the structure of an XML document and provides a list of elements and attributes that may constitute that structure and where and how they may be used within the document.

Tutorial website: http://www.w3schools.com/dtd/default.asp

EAC-CPF: Encoded Archival Context–Corporate Bodies, Persons, and Families

EAC-CPF is an XML schema that serves as a framework for communicating description of the individuals, groups, and institutions that create, collect, and preserve and are the subject of archival materials. A beta version of the data structure standard was released in 2004. The standard was adopted by SAA in 2011 and is maintained by SAA's EAC Working Group, in partnership with the Berlin State Library.

Website: http://eac.staatsbibliothek-berlin.de/

EAD: Encoded Archival Description
EAD is an archival data structure standard, encoded in XML, that was developed by the archival community and released in 1997. The standard was revised in 2002 and is currently undergoing a second process of review by SAA's Technical Subcommittee on EAD (TS-EAD).
Website: http://www.loc.gov/ead/

FRBR: Functional Requirements for Bibliographic Records
FRBR is a model for bibliographic description that is based on entities and the relationships between them, rather than a traditional bibliographic model exemplified in ISBD. FRBR is the model for Resource Description and Access (RDA), slated to replace AACR2 as the bibliographic content standard in the United States.
Website: http://www.ifla.org/files/cataloguing/frbr/frbr_2008.pdf

HTML: Hypertext Markup Language
HTML is a language used to mark up documents for the Web. A browser will use the instructions in an HTML document to create a Web page. The latest version of HTML is HTML5, released in 2012.
Tutorial website: http://www.w3schools.com/html/default.asp

ICA-AtoM
ICA-AtoM is an open-source, Web-based archival data management software program based on ICA descriptive standards and supported by Artefactual Systems and the Program Commission of the International Council on Archives (ICA). It is widely used internationally.
Website: https://www.ica-atom.org

ICA-ISDF: International Standard for Describing Functions
This ICA-supported data content standard captures information about the functions performed by records creators that result in the creation of records. This standard was approved by ICA in 2008.
Website: http://www.wien2004.ica.org/en/node/38665

ICA-ISDIAH: International Standard for Describing Institutions with Archival Holdings

This ICA-supported data content standard was originally adopted by that organization in 2008. ISDIAH captures information about the institutions at which archival materials are stored and may be accessed.
Website: http://www.wien2004.ica.org/en/node/38884

ILS: Integrated Library Systems

Integrated library systems allow library assets to be tracked by patrons and staff. They usually incorporate multiple user interfaces (depending on the type of user—whether patron or staff) with a database that holds information about the library assets. ILSs may be open source, such as Greenstone or Koha, or proprietary, such as Aleph (from Ex Libris).

ISAAR(CPF): International Standard Archival Authority Record (Corporate Bodies, Persons, and Families)

This ICA-supported data content standard was originally published in 1996 and revised in 2003. It is a standard for archival authority records that describe the institutions, individuals, and groups that create, maintain, and are the subject of archival materials.
Website: http://www.icacds.org/uk/eng/ISAAR(CPF)2ed.pdf

ISAD(G): General International Standard Archival Description

This ICA-supported data content standard was originally adopted by that organization in 1993 and revised in 1999. The standard provides basic guidance on describing archival materials and is modelled on the ICA-supported bibliographic standard ISBD(G). DACS, widely used in the United States as a data content standard for archival description, is based on the principles set forth in ISAD(G).
Website: http://www.icacds.org/uk/eng/ISAD(G).pdf

ISBD(G): General International Standard Bibliographic Description

First published in 1977 and compiled by the International Federation of Library Associations (IFLA) Committee on Cataloging, ISBD(G) provides an international content standard for description of all types of library materials. The standard was revised in 1992 and again in 2004.
Website: http://www.ifla.org/files/cataloguing/isbd/isbd-g_2004.pdf

LCNAF: Library of Congress Name Authority File
LCNAF is a data value standard maintained by the Library of Congress that provides authority files for individuals, corporate bodies, events, places, and titles. Authority files are submitted by contributing organizations and are largely derived from bibliographic descriptions. This standard is used in bibliographic and archival description.
Website: http://id.loc.gov/authorities/names.html

LCSH: Library of Congress Subject Headings
LCSH is a data value standard first published in 1898 and maintained by the Library of Congress that provides a structured and controlled vocabulary for subjects and their subdivisions. This standard is used in bibliographic and archival description.
Website: http://id.loc.gov/authorities/subjects.html

MADS: Metadata Authority Description Schema
MADS is an XML schema for authority records (for individuals, topics, and genres) and is supported by the Library of Congress. It is a companion standard to MODS and provides information about the entities described in MODS.
Website: http://www.loc.gov/standards/mads/

MARBI: Machine-Readable Bibliographic Information
MARBI is an interdivisional committee of the ALA that, notably, voted in 1988 to combine MARC standards for various formats into a single MARC record for multiple formats. More generally, the committee reviews and recommends machine-readable standards for bibliographic description.
Website: http://www.ala.org/alcts/mgrps/cmtes/jnt-marbi

MARC: Machine-Readable Cataloging
MARC is a data structure standard developed by librarians in the 1960s to provide a standard structure to organize the information needed to describe bibliographic materials. The format consists of a record composed of data elements, or categories of information, such as title, author, date, and subject.
Website: http://www.loc.gov/marc/

MARC 21: A format for bibliographic data
Released in 1999, MARC 21 merged the United States MARC format with the Canadian MARC format. MARC 21 was last updated in September 2012 (update 15).
Website: http://www.loc.gov/marc/bibliographic/

MARC AMC: Machine-Readable Cataloging for Archives and Manuscripts Control/Archives and Mixed Collections
In the early 1980s the National Information Systems Task Force (NISTF), a group appointed by SAA, created a version of MARC specifically for describing archival materials, called the MARC Format for Manuscripts and Archival Control (MARC AMC), which later became the MARC Format for Archives and Mixed Collections. MARC AMC gave archivists the ability to describe collections briefly and in a way that allowed them to be retrievable with other bibliographic records in a library catalog.

MARCXML
MARCXML is an XML schema for MARC 21 records.
Website: http://www.loc.gov/standards/marcxml

METS: Metadata Encoding and Descriptive Standard
METS is an XML encoding standard for structural data maintained by the Library of Congress. METS captures the information necessary to render complex digital objects and the relationships between the files that make up that object.
Website: http://www.loc.gov/standards/mets/

MIX: Metadata for Images in XML
MIX is an XML schema often used for capturing technical metadata for digital images, such as color space and compression type.
Website: http://www.loc.gov/standards/mix/

MODS: Metadata Object Description Schema
MODS is an XML standard to describe digital objects. MODS data elements constitute a subset of the MARC data element set and use language-based tags (instead of the numeric tags employed by MARCXML), employ attributes to refine elements, and allow for hierarchical relationships between elements.
Website: http://www.loc.gov/standards/mods

Standards for Archival Description

NACO: Name Authority Cooperative Program
This program trains catalogers from participating institutions in the process of forming and contributing authority records to LCNAF. SACO performs the same function for LCSH.
Websites: http://www.loc.gov/aba/pcc/naco/ and http://www.loc.gov/aba/pcc/saco/index.html

NISTF: National Information Systems Task Force
In the early 1980s the NISTF, a group appointed by SAA, created a version of MARC specifically for describing archival materials, called MARC AMC.

NUCMC: National Union Catalog of Manuscript Collections
From 1959 to 1993, the Library of Congress produced NUCMC as print catalogs of collection-level archival descriptions from repositories across the country. These catalogs are still available on microfilm, although catalogers now create basic authority records and collection-level MARC 21 records for use in OCLC WorldCat.
Website: http://www.loc.gov/coll/nucmc/

NWDA: Northwest Digital Archives
Begun in 2002, NWDA represents a consortium of archival repositories located in the northwestern United States that provides access through a single Web interface to a shared index of EAD finding aids.
Website: http://nwda.orbiscascade.org

OAC: Online Archive of California
Established in 2002, the OAC represents a consortium of archival repositories located in California that provides access through a single Web interface to archival collection descriptions and digital objects via a shared index of EAD finding aids. The OAC is supported by the University of California system.
Website: http://www.oac.cdlib.org/

OAI-PMH: Open Archives Initiative Protocol for Metadata Harvesting
OAI-PMH is a standard for metadata exchange between repositories.
Website: http://www.openarchives.org/pmh/

OAIS: Open Archival Information System
OAIS is an ISO standard that describes a model for preserving certain types of digital information and making it available to designated communities. The standard was first published in 2003 and was revised in 2012. The model specifies frameworks for shared terms, preservation strategies, and the architecture of storage systems.
Website: http://public.ccsds.org/publications/archive/650x0m2.pdf

PBCore
PBCore is a metadata schema based on Dublin Core and extended for richer description of media materials. PBCore is predominantly used in the public broadcasting community; in fact, the Public Broadcasting Corporation funded development of the standard. Initially released in 2007, the most recent version (2.0) was released in 2011.
Website: http://pbcore.org/index.php

PREMIS: Preservation Metadata: Implementation Strategies
PREMIS is the most commonly used preservation metadata standard for digital objects. PREMIS may be expressed in XML or RDF. The PREMIS data dictionary, which defines the semantic units that constitute the data model, was initially released in 2005 by a working group convened by RLG and OCLC. Version 2.2 of the standard was released in 2012 by the PREMIS Editorial Committee, which is sponsored by the Library of Congress.
Website: http://www.loc.gov/standards/premis/

RAD: Rules for Archival Description
This data content standard is the Canadian equivalent of DACS. Like DACS, it is based on ISAD(G). The standard is maintained by the Canadian Committee on Archival Description.
Website: http://www.cdncouncilarchives.ca/RAD/RADComplete_July2008.pdf

RDA: Resource Description and Access
RDA is a bibliographic content standard designed to replace AACR2. Developed by the Joint Steering Committee for the Development of RDA and co-published by the ALA, the Canadian Library Association, and Facet Publishing, RDA is intended to cover various formats and types of content. The Library of Congress will implement RDA as its cataloging standard in 2013. (Note: The full standard in its final version is not available online; you must purchase a print edition or subscribe to the RDA Toolkit [http://www.rdatoolkit.org].)
Website: http://www.rda-jsc.org/rdafulldraft.html

RDF: Resource Description Framework
RDF is a W3C standard for data exchange on the Web. RDF employs URIs to convey not only nodes of information but also the links between nodes, often referred to as "triples."
Website: http://www.w3.org/RDF/

SNAC: Social Networks and Archival Context Project
SNAC is a collaborative project between the University of Virginia; University of California, Berkeley; and the California Digital Library that seeks to derive EAC-CPF records from existing EAD records; match those names to other EAD records as well as name records in authority files like LCNAF, ULAN, and the Virtual International Authority File (VIAF); winnow out duplicate names; and match name variants with each other.
Website: http://socialarchive.iath.virginia.edu/

SPARQL: SPARQL Protocol and RDF Query Language
SPARQL is a query language allowing a user or application to retrieve or manipulate data stored in the RDF format.
Website: http://www.w3.org/TR/rdf-sparql-query

TARO: Texas Archival Resources Online
TARO is a consortial project providing access to many finding aids at many Texas repositories.
Website: http://www.lib.utexas.edu/taro/index.html

TGN: Thesaurus of Geographic Names
First published in 1997, the Thesaurus of Geographic Names is a data value standard compiled by the Getty that provides a controlled vocabulary for concepts relating to the description of geographic locations and features, including both physical and political divisions.
Website: http://www.getty.edu/research/tools/vocabularies/tgn/index.html

TS-DACS: Technical Subcommittee on DACS
Website: http://www2.archivists.org/groups/technical-subcommittee-on-describing-archives-a-content-standard-dacs

TS-EAD: Technical Subcommittee on EAD
Website: http://www2.archivists.org/groups/technical-subcommittee-on-encoded-archival-description-ead

ULAN: Union List of Artist Names
First published in 1994, the Thesaurus of Geographic Names is a data value standard compiled by the Getty that provides a controlled vocabulary for artist names (individuals and groups).
Website: http://www.getty.edu/research/tools/vocabularies/ulan/index.html

URI: Uniform Resource Identifier
A URI identifies a single Web document or other resource. Web document URIs return representations of a resource in response to Hypertext Transfer Protocol (HTTP) requests. Semantic Web URIs identify not just documents, but real-world objects such as people, places, and things and also intangible things, like ideas.
Website: http://www.w3.org/Addressing/URL/URI_Overview.html and http://www.w3.org/TR/cooluris/#oldweb

VIAF: Virtual International Authority File
Hosted by OCLC, VIAF is a project to link authority files from several national libraries and regional or transnational associations, making the files available on the Web.
Website: http://www.oclc.org/viaf

XML: Extensible Markup Language
XML is based on Standard Generalized Markup Language (SGML) and is a standard markup language for the World Wide Web. XML is a standard for data exchange widely used outside of libraries, archives, and museums. XML provides a great deal of flexibility in data manipulation and transformation.
Tutorial website: http://www.w3schools.com/xml

XSD: XML Schema Document
An XML schema is a model document that defines the structure of a class or group of XML documents. The XSD sets forth the rules for a valid document according to that schema.
Tutorial website: http://www.w3schools.com/schema/default.asp

XSL: Extensible Stylesheet Language
XSL is a stylesheet language for XML documents—XSL defines how XML documents should be displayed on the Web.
Tutorial website: http://www.w3schools.com/xsl/

XSLT: Extensible Stylesheet Language Transformations
XSLT is a language that transforms XML documents into HTML or into other XML documents.
Website: http://www.w3.org/TR/xslt

XTF: Extensible Text Framework
XTF is an open-source application that can index and sort XML documents and display them on the Web via XSLT. It was developed in 2010 and is maintained by the California Digital Library.
Website: http://xtf.cdlib.org

MODULE 2
PROCESSING DIGITAL RECORDS AND MANUSCRIPTS

J. Gordon Daines III

Table of Contents

Introduction • 90

Issues and Challenges Posed by
Digital Records and Manuscripts • 91

Arrangement and Description:
Mapping a Business Process • 100
    Accessioning • 101
    Gathering Contextual Information • 102
    Performing a Conservation Assessment • 103
    Providing an Arrangement Scheme/Intellectual Arrangement • 104
    Arranging the Records • 105
    Describing the Records • 107
    Creating Access Tools • 108
    Sample Processing Workflow • 109

Digital Processing: Practices
and Procedures • 111
    Using the OAIS Reference Model • 111
    Preparing to Process • 113
    Developing Policies and Procedures • 114
    Accessioning • 115
    Arrangement and Description • 120

Recommendations • 125

Appendices
  Appendix A: Case Studies
    Duke University: David M. Rubenstein Rare Book
      & Manuscript Library • 129
      by Seth Shaw
    Brigham Young University Archives:
      Sidney B. Sperry Photographs • 131
      by J. Gordon Daines III
  Appendix B: Recent and Current Activities • 133
  Appendix C: Selected Tools for Use in Processing
    Digital Records and Manuscripts • 137
  Appendix D: Standards Applicable to the Description of
    Digital Records and Manuscripts • 141
  Appendix E: Further Reading • 142

ABOUT THE AUTHOR

J. Gordon Daines III is the university archivist and assistant department chair, manuscripts, in the L. Tom Perry Special Collections at Brigham Young University. He holds degrees in history from Brigham Young University (BA) and the University of Chicago (MA) and a certificate in archives and records management from Western Washington University. His research interests include the history of Brigham Young University, the history of the archival profession in Utah, dealing with digital records, digital preservation, and business process management as applied to archives.

Introduction

The last two decades have seen the development of remarkable technologies that enable people and institutions to create, store, copy, and manage their information in electronic systems. This fact has important implications for the work of archivists and curators, because much of this information provides evidence of organizational or personal activities, but relatively little of it ever exists in print form. As we move deeper into the twenty-first century, it is vital that we develop the skills necessary for acquiring and managing digital records and manuscripts in a way that preserves their value as evidence and information. Such skills will become an increasingly large part of our profession.

The 2012 report *AIMS Born-Digital Collections: An Inter-Institutional Model for Stewardship* acknowledges that "the challenges of stewarding born-digital material demand new strategies as well as a redefinition of archival workflows."[1] This task is not as imposing as it first seems. Archivists can use many existing and emerging tools to help them redefine archival workflows to accommodate digital records and manuscripts. Concepts from the business community, such as business process modeling and process mapping, can help us understand where tasks can be left the same and where they need to be re-engineered.[2]

The Society of American Archivists' *Glossary of Archival and Records Terminology* defines archival processing as "the arrangement, description, and housing of archival materials for storage and use by patrons."[3] Digital records and manuscripts force an important adjustment to this traditional definition of archival processing. By carefully examining existing processing strategies and by adapting new tools and services in light of the demands that digital materials impose, archivists can exercise appropriate stewardship over electronic records and collections.

---

1 AIMS Work Group, *AIMS Born-Digital Collections: An Inter-Institutional Model for Stewardship*, 2001, p. I, accessed March 14, 2012, http://www2.lib.virginia.edu/aims/whitepaper/AIMS_final.pdf.
2 J. Gordon Daines III, "Re-engineering Archives: Business Process Management (BPM) and the Quest for Archival Efficiency," *American Archivist* 74 (Spring/Summer 2011): 124–159.
3 Richard Pearce-Moses, *A Glossary of Archival and Records Terminology* (Chicago: Society of American Archivists, 2005), accessed July 17, 2012, http://www2.archivists.org/glossary.

This module discusses workflows, procedures, and tools that can facilitate archival control over such materials. It comprises four sections plus appendices. The first examines the challenges and opportunities that digital records and manuscripts pose for archivists. The second section discusses how and why archival processing workflows can be adjusted in order to accommodate digital records and manuscripts. It describes how each archival process will be affected by the acquisition of born-digital records. It also lists the steps that constitute archival processing of such materials. The third section provides practical guidance on how archivists can manage the digital records and manuscripts in their stewardship, including a description of specific tools and sample workflows that facilitate such work. The fourth section consists of recommendations for developing the skills necessary for dealing with digital records and manuscripts. The module assumes a working knowledge of the basic principles of archival arrangement and description as described in Kathleen D. Roe's book *Arranging and Describing Archives and Manuscripts*.[4]

Issues and Challenges Posed by Digital Records and Manuscripts

Archivists have long recognized the challenges and opportunities posed by digital records and manuscripts. In 1984 Thomas Elton Brown wrote an article describing how the Society of American Archivists (SAA) was beginning to tackle the challenges posed by the computer. Brown described how SAA's formal involvement with the issues surrounding machine-readable records began in 1967 as a co-sponsor of the National Symposium on the Impact of Automation on Documentation. He also described SAA-sponsored activities that could help archivists tackle electronic records. Brown's conclusion noted some of the problems identified by the SAA Task Force on Automated Records and Techniques that challenged archivists in the early 1980s: "[T]he task force acknowledged that little work has been undertaken to solve the archival problems with recent technological innovations. These include database management systems, microprocessors,

---

4   Kathleen D. Roe, *Arranging and Describing Archives and Manuscripts* (Chicago: Society of American Archivists, 2005).

digitized textual information, computerized cartographic information dependent on plotter hardware, optical digital data disk technology, and transborder data flow questions."[5]

Echoes of Brown's concern can be heard from archivists today. Christopher A. Lee and Helen Tibbo stated in 2011 that "efforts to further articulate and define the characteristics of digital curation have come at the same time that the archival profession faces unprecedented opportunities and challenges related to electronic records."[6] Adrian Cunningham believes that archivists need to learn to negotiate "the ongoing evolution of digital lives and the opportunities/challenges for capturing and managing the digital evidence of those lives in all their manifestations."[7] Peter Williams, Jeremy Leighton John, and Ian Rowland have pointed out that the field of personal information management is "a rich field for research, as there are still major gaps in our knowledge, especially in regard to the strategies that individuals use to organize and manage their personal digital archives."[8]

Managing digital manuscripts and records is a new proposition for many archivists, and the literature acknowledges the challenges that archivists face in dealing with these materials. The issues posed by digital records provide archivists the opportunity to engage more intimately with those involved with the creation and management of digital manuscripts and records, to develop digital curation competencies, to capture and manage contextual information, and to gather the technical metadata that facilitates the appropriate management of digital records and manuscripts over time.

The ability to customize and personalize digital materials means that "collecting institutions may need to inquire how the donor managed his or her digital content, approached data transfer between computers, and used applications, directories, and tools."[9] Adrian

---

5 Thomas Elton Brown, "The Society of American Archivists Confronts the Computer," *American Archivist* 47 (Fall 1984): 382.
6 Christopher A. Lee and Helen Tibbo, "Where's the Archivist in Digital Curation? Exploring the Possibilities through a Matrix of Knowledge and Skills," *Archivaria* 72 (Fall 2011): 126.
7 Adrian Cunningham, "Ghosts in the Machine: Towards a Principles-Based Approach to Making and Keeping Digital Personal Records," in *I, Digital: Personal Collections in the Digital Era*, ed. Christopher A. Lee (Chicago: Society of American Archivists, 2011): 79.
8 Peter Williams, Jeremy Leighton John, and Ian Rowland, "The Personal Curation of Digital Objects: A Lifecycle Approach," *Aslib Proceedings: New Information Perspectives* 61, no. 4 (2009): 357.
9 Laura Carroll, Erika Farr, Peter Hornsby, and Ben Ranker, "A Comprehensive Approach to Born-Digital Archives," *Archivaria* 72 (Fall 2011): 73.

Cunningham has argued similarly that "if digital archiving is to succeed, it must include intervention in the creation and management of digital information."[10] Precustodial work provides archivists an opportunity to deepen relationships with the donors and creators of the materials held in their collections. These relationships allow for the gathering of information that enhances and enriches our ability to appropriately care for digital materials. Archivists can ask donors and creators how they generated the digital materials that they are donating to the archives, for what purpose the materials were created, and how they managed those materials. This information is useful not only in determining how the digital manuscripts and records will be stored; it can also be used to describe the materials so that researchers will be able to access them and future archivists will be able to manage them.

The long-term preservation of digital manuscripts and records presents archivists with another growth opportunity as they become more familiar with the technical solutions available for managing digital materials. Over the last two decades, archivists have begun to take steps to familiarize themselves with these technical solutions, as a digital preservation literature has emerged in the major archival journals.[11] Henry M. Gladney has written that "for professional and social reasons, we want to deploy infrastructure for preserving digital content whatsoever in ways that meet the needs of its eventual users."[12] His article describes how archivists can take existing technologies and adapt them to meet archival needs.

In his article "Bridging the Gap," Ben Goldman presents practical recommendations that archivists can use to begin managing digital records and manuscripts, given their existing skills and available technologies. He recommends that archivists begin small, by conducting an inventory of the digital materials in their institution—a process that is familiar to most archivists who have surveyed paper-

---

10 Adrian Cunningham, "Digital Curation/Digital Archiving: A View from the National Archives of Australia," *American Archivist* 71 (Fall/Winter 2008): 535.
11 For example, see Lisa M. Schmidt, "Preserving the H-Net Email Lists: A Case Study in Trusted Digital Repository Assessment," *American Archivist* 74 (Spring/Summer 2011): 257–296; Michael Forstrum, "Managing Electronic Records in Manuscript Collections: A Case Study from the Beinecke Rare Book and Manuscript Library," *American Archivist* 72 (Fall/Winter 2009): 460–477; Carroll, Farr, Hornsby, and Ranker, "Comprehensive Approach"; and Ciaran B. Trace, "Beyond the Magic to the Mechanism: Computers, Materiality, and What It Means for Records to Be 'Born Digital,'" *Archivaria* 72 (Fall 2011): 5–27.
12 Henry M. Gladney, "Long-Term Preservation of Digital Records: Trustworthy Digital Objects," *American Archivist* 72 (Fall/Winter 2009): 434.

based archives. Once the inventory has been completed, archivists should choose and implement a consistent storage service for digital records and manuscripts, keeping, "at a minimum, two separate instances of storage . . . one for archival masters, and one for access copies." The notion of archival masters and access copies is another one that is familiar to archivists—it has been used with microfilm for decades. Goldman also recommends that archivists formulate policies to guide future acquisition and preservation activities.[13] His article is one example of how archivists are beginning to engage more fully with the concepts of digital curation and how they are adapting existing practices in order to develop the skills that can help us preserve digital content.

Digital curation means much more than simply placing digital records and manuscripts on storage media—it involves a wide range of processes that are applied to those materials over the course of their lifecycle. Ross Harvey has argued that the proper management of digital manuscripts and records requires more than a focus on maintaining and preserving digital information. Archivists also need to pay attention to "what comes before preservation and what comes after—that is, how the data are created and how they are used before they get to an archive or library and how they will be used, and by whom, in the future."[14] Adrian Cunningham has similarly argued that "just as archival operations are more than preservation, digital archives are more than digital preservation."[15]

Both Harvey and Cunningham posit that archivists need to develop skills in digital curation. Digital curation has been defined as "maintaining, preserving and adding value to digital research data throughout its lifecycle."[16] One of the crucial concepts of digital curation is adding value to the digital records and manuscripts that archivists acquire. This is done through the addition of metadata that facilitates the reuse and proper management of the digital records

---

13 Ben Goldman, "Bridging the Gap: Taking Practical Steps Toward Managing Born-Digital Collections in Manuscript Repositories," *RBM: A Journal of Rare Books, Manuscripts, and Cultural Heritage* 12, no. 1 (March 2011): 11–24.
14 Ross Harvey, *Digital Curation: A How-To-Do-It Manual* (New York: Neal-Schuman Publishers, 2004), xvi.
15 Cunningham, "Digital Curation/Digital Archiving," 540.
16 "What Is Digital Curation?," Digital Curation Centre, accessed March 23, 2012, http://www.dcc.ac.uk/digital-curation/what-digital-curation.

and manuscripts.¹⁷ Creating metadata is something that archivists have done for years with the creation of finding aids, catalog records, and, more recently, digital object metadata to facilitate the creation, management, and discovery of digitized archival materials.

Digital curation pushes archivists to become proactive early in the lifecycle of digital manuscripts and records. Much of the metadata used by archivists to add value to the digital records and manuscripts is best captured before it comes to the archives.

Deeper involvement with the lifecycle of digital manuscripts and records allows archivists to gather the detailed contextual information that will aid future users of the materials. This point is well illustrated by Sabine Mas, Dominique Maurel, and Inge Alberts in their article, "Applying Faceted Classification to the Personal Organization of Electronic Records." The authors discuss how individuals operating within organizational structures manage their digital manuscripts and records. They found that "although institutional classification schemes are intended to facilitate the organization of records for the short or long term as well as the localization and retrieval of these records by all users, employees rarely use this type of tool to organize and retrieve electronic records that are saved on their workstations."¹⁸ Their findings resonate with the research coming out of the personal information management literature. This research describes two basic ways that people locate their digital records and manuscripts. To locate materials, individuals either

1. use native search functionality to locate materials on their computers; or
2. browse or navigate through the tree structures created by their computers.

A large number of people rely on a search to locate or relocate their digital records and manuscripts.¹⁹ Such strategies succeed only

---

17 The SAA *Glossary* defines *metadata* as "a characterization or description documenting the identification, management, nature, use, or location of information resources (data)." Archivists use several different types of metadata. They include administrative metadata, descriptive metadata, preservation metadata, and structural metadata. See Pearce-Moses, *Glossary*.
18 Sabine Mas, Dominique Maurel, and Inge Alberts, "Applying Faceted Classification to the Personal Organization of Electronic Records: Insights into the User Experience," *Archivaria* 72 (Fall 2011): 30.
19 For a good introductory essay describing personal information management, see Christopher A. Lee and Robert Capra, "And Now the Twain Shall Meet: Exploring the Connections Between PIM and Archives," in *I, Digital: Personal Collections in the Digital Era*, ed. Christopher A. Lee (Chicago: Society of American Archivists, 2011), 29–77.

because the native search applications are able to take advantage of native file metadata or, in some cases, an index of each file's full text, which is typically maintained by the host operating system. Archivists must be able to describe the software and hardware used to generate digital manuscripts and records, as well as the evolving sets of tools that records creators use to organize and locate those digital manuscripts and records. Future users will also benefit from understanding how creators leveraged those search tools in their own work, and such information can be recorded as part of the descriptive records.

Archivists will also need to provide search mechanisms for contextual information about preserved records. Contextual information is one critical means by which users discover and interpret digital manuscripts and records held by an archival repository. Archivists must understand how such information can be indexed and searched via discovery tools implemented by the repository, such as those discussed by Daniel A. Santamaria in Module 3, *Designing Descriptive and Access Systems*.[20]

The final challenge and opportunity addressed in this module is the need for archivists to gather additional metadata describing digital materials, in particular, technical metadata. Archivists have built a strong apparatus for gathering and managing the descriptive information necessary to locate and use physical manuscripts and records that are relevant to a particular research need. The growing importance of digital manuscripts and records means that archivists will have to augment that apparatus with technical metadata about those digital materials in their collections. It is very difficult to properly manage digital materials without proper technical metadata. It is equally difficult to provide access to those materials without technical metadata. Digital records and manuscripts are created using specific software and hardware. In many cases these materials are unusable without the correct software and hardware. Technical metadata describes what software and hardware was used to create the digital materials. It tracks file formats, resolutions, color profiles, and other information identifying a file's type and characterizing its

---

20 Daniel A. Santamaria, *Designing Descriptive and Access Systems* (Chicago: Society of American Archivists, 2013) is Module 3 in Trends in Archives Practice that complements the volume by Kathleen Roe, *Arranging and Describing Archives and Manuscripts* (Chicago: Society of American Archivists, 2005).

content. Recording this information in a consistent fashion will enable the materials to be accessed, rendered, and used in the future.

Tools that will help archivists identify and gather appropriate technical metadata include PRONOM, UDFR, DROID, JHOVE, and JHOVE2.[21] PRONOM and UDFR are file registries; DROID is a desktop tool that allows archivists to identify what format the digital record or manuscript claims to be by referencing the PRONOM database.[22] JHOVE and JHOVE2 allow archivists to verify that a digital record or manuscript is what it purports to be and to characterize some aspects of its content. The importance of appropriate metadata, including technical metadata, is a recurring theme in Ross Harvey's digital curation manual, and the archival profession is well on its way to becoming more comfortable identifying and gathering appropriate technical metadata using tools such as those listed above and in this module's Appendix C.

When working with hybrid (that is to say, mixed analog and digital) collections, archivists face challenges similar to those they confront when processing digital-only collections. The digital records and manuscripts contained in hybrid collections need to be managed in a similar fashion to digital-only materials held by the collecting repository, but hybrid collections pose a unique challenge: the need to integrate information about the digital and physical components of materials related by their provenance. Archivists also need to manage information about the storage locations of both the physical and the digital components of collections so that appropriate access can be provided to patrons. Archivists intellectually can unite all of the components of a hybrid collection or they can describe the digital materials separately from the physical materials; the precise methods to be used should be aligned with institutional capacities and policies.

In 2000, Anne Gilliland-Swetland argued that intellectually integrating the digital records and manuscripts with the physical materials provided an important way to understand the materials. She

---

21 More information about JHOVE is available at http://hul.harvard.edu/johove. More information about JHOVE2 is available at https://bitbucket.org/jhove2/main/wiki/Home. More information about PRONOM is available at http://www.nationalarchives.gov.uk/PRONOM/Default.aspx. More information about DROID is available at http://droid.sourceforge.net.

22 It is important to note that the Unified Digital Format Registry (UDFR) was recently released and that it supercedes PRONOM and GRFR. Information about UDFR is available at http://www.udfr.org/.

posited that "the archival approach offers the concepts of collective arrangement and description according to the provenance of the materials; these provide benefits even when information managers or users are not interested in the evidential value of the materials. Applying these concepts makes it possible to unite related digital, nondigital, and predigital materials according to their intellectual rather than their physical characteristics. These concepts build context, which is a powerful and underused tool for facilitating understanding and ultimately creating knowledge."[23]

The Harry Ransom Center has attempted to apply this concept in their handling of hybrid collections. Their approach has been "holistic: the digital archivist not only preserves the computer files but also organizes and describes the entirety of a collection by integrating paper and digital materials."[24] Catherine Stollar Peters elaborates further on this practice in her article about how the Michael Joyce papers were described at the Ransom Center. She writes that "although his electronic and paper materials would be housed separately, we chose to arrange all of his materials using the same functional series, as opposed to series based on format, to demonstrate the original order in which Michael Joyce created his papers."[25] This approach follows sound archival principles and practices while adapting them to new realities. It allows the descriptive records to help researchers understand the intellectual arrangement of the hybrid collection while also acknowledging that the digital manuscripts and records of the Joyce collection need to be managed and stored differently than the physical materials.

Arguments have also been made that because digital materials need to be stored and managed differently from physical materials, they should be arranged and described as distinct components of an archival collection, with the functional relationship to nondigital materials defined at the collection level. Archivists at Stanford University

---

23 Anne J. Gilliland-Swetland, *Enduring Paradigm, New Opportunities: The Value of the Archival Perspective in the Digital Environment* (Washington, DC: Council on Library and Information Resources, February 2000), 14, accessed March 23, 2012, http://www.clir.org/pubs/reports/pub89/pub89.pdf.

24 Matthew G. Kirschenbaum et al., "Approaches to Managing and Collecting Born-Digital Literary Materials for Scholarly Use," white paper for the NEH Office of Digital Humanities, May 2009, p. 11.

25 Catherine Stollar Peters, "When Not All Papers Are Paper: A Case Study in Digital Archivy," *Provenance* 24 (2006): 28.

opted to take this approach when they chose to separately describe the physical and digital materials in the Robert Creeley papers.[26] They created a Computer Files series that is part of the overall descriptive apparatus for the collection. The Computer Files series contains the electronic records created by Creeley. This is also a reasonable approach that follows sound archival principles and practices while adapting them to new realities. It allows the descriptive records to help researchers discover the digital materials. It also recognizes the reality that the digital materials need to be stored, managed, and provided to patrons differently than the physical materials. If this approach is used, an archivist should record descriptive notes in the collection level record, clearly explaining the relationship of the digital materials to the non-digital parts of the collection.

As Christopher A. Lee and Helen Tibbo acknowledge in the development of the DigCCur Matrix and Curriculum, traditional archival principles, skills, and knowledge play a central and foundational role in how archivists will tackle the challenges and opportunities presented by digital manuscripts and records. However, these traditional principles, skills, and knowledge are "by themselves not sufficient for expressing the full range of digital curation activities to be performed."[27] The need to adapt traditional archival practice to meet the needs of the digital age is a common theme in the archival literature.[28] The next section examines how business process mapping can be used to understand how the traditional archival processing routines can be adjusted to meet current archival needs. Based on the unique needs of digital records, some concepts and practices can remain the same and other concepts and practices will need to be adjusted. The section concludes with a discussion of one potential method to re-engineering archival processing to better manage digital records and manuscripts.

---

26 AIMS Work Group, *AIMS Born-Digital Collections*, 88–90.
27 Lee and Tibbo, "Where's the Archivist in Digital Curation?," 130.
28 For deeper discussion of the need to adapt traditional archival practices to the digital age, see the works cited above by Lee and Tibbo; Gilliland-Swetland; Chris Hilton and Dave Thompson, "Collecting Born Digital Archives at the Wellcome Library," *Ariadne* 50 (January 2007), accessed March 22, 2012, http://www.ariadne.ac.uk/issue50/hilton-thompson; and Carroll, Farr, Hornsby, and Ranker.

Arrangement and Description: Mapping a Business Process

A crucial step for moving archival processing practices into the digital realm is to clearly understand the current workflows and steps that the repository is using for analog records. The particular practices used by a repository should reflect the following description of archival processing, which is drawn largely from Chapter 4 of *Arranging & Describing Archives & Manuscripts*.[29] This section highlights areas of archival processing that archivists will need to adjust or completely re-engineer so that they can successfully manage digital records and manuscripts. The application of the various tasks and sub-tasks described as part of the archival processing business process will vary from institution to institution. This section concludes with a sample re-engineering of the steps of archival processing that has the potential to enable archivists to better manage digital records and manuscripts.

The archival processing business process involves seven tasks.[30] Once records appraisal has been completed and records have been received by an archives, these steps traditionally occur in the following order:

- accessioning records;
- gathering contextual information about the records;
- performing a conservation assessment;
- establishing an arrangement scheme/intellectual arrangement;
- arranging the records physically, if necessary;
- describing the records; and
- creating access tools.

Each of these tasks can be broken into sub-tasks that enable archivists to accomplish the business process of arranging and describing records. Examining these tasks and subtasks at a summary level is an essential first step, allowing archivists to adjust their archival processing workflows so that they can manage digital records and manuscripts in light of institutional needs and requirements.

---

29 Roe, *Arranging and Describing Archives and Manuscripts*, 45–97.
30 A business process is "a series of interrelated activities, crossing functional boundaries, with specific inputs and outputs." It is the series of steps or tasks necessary to complete archival processing. Understanding what these tasks are and the way that they are interconnected enables us to examine whether or not they need to be changed when dealing with digital records and manuscripts. More information on business processes can be found in Colin Armistead and Simon Machin, "Business Process Management: Implications for Productivity in Multi-State Service Networks," *International Journal of Service Industry Management* 9, no. 4 (1998): 323–326. The quote in this footnote is on p. 324.

Accessioning

Traditionally, accessioning is the first task that is directly relevant to archival processing. During accessioning, an archivist takes physical and legal custody of a body of records or manuscripts. Basic information is recorded to document the nature and extent of the material received by the archives, as well as its source. The accessioning task typically comprises four sub-tasks:

- taking physical and administrative control of the materials;
- reviewing the content and condition of the materials;
- creating case files to manage information about the accession; and
- identifying the arrangement and description priority of the materials.

The sub-task most impacted by digital records and manuscripts is that of taking physical control of the materials. The key lies in taking custody in a way that preserves the authenticity of the digital records and manuscripts. It is acceptable to receive material in a number of ways. These include direct transfer from the donor using media (CDs, DVDs, flash drives, floppy disks, etc.), FTP transfer, or use of utilities like Box and Dropbox (online backup and file-sharing services). Acceptable methods also include capture directly from a donor's computer and/or capture from a server where the donor might be hosting a website or internal files. Materials received directly from the donor need to be removed immediately to a sustainable format. At the most basic level, this can be done using a file transfer program like Teracopy.[31] Teracopy is designed to transfer large numbers of files quickly. It generates checksum values, verifies successful transfers, and presents the user with a list of potentially corrupted files.[32] Utilities such as Robocopy and RichCopy offer other robust file copying options.

While it is easy to copy or move files using file system tools such as those listed above, an archivist should be aware that when transfer is made with file-system tools, the copying process may skip hidden files or technical metadata. Disk imaging software such as Clonezilla, FTK

---

31 More information on Teracopy is available at http://codesector.com/teracopy.
32 A checksum is a fixed-size datum computed from an arbitrary block of digital data for the purpose of detecting accidental errors that may have been introduced during transmission or storage.

Imager, or the Mac Disk Utility can be used to capture a bit-by-bit copy of data from computer hard drives or other media. Disk imaging will preserve more metadata than simple file copying, but it requires the use of more advanced tools to extract the files and to make them useful.

For files that cannot be transferred easily from a user's computer, other options are available. Web harvesting tools or database backup utilities can be used to capture materials from servers. Tools such as Aid4Mail, Mailstore Home, and Offline IMAP can be used to capture e-mail. These tools should be used in conjunction with checksum generators such as MD5 checker to ensure that the technical metadata associated with the files is accurate and that files have not changed during the transfer process. These checksums can also be used to authenticate the digital records and manuscripts at a later date.

The sub-task of reviewing content and condition of materials also needs to be adapted for the unique needs of digital records and manuscripts. An archivist should create a working copy of the digital materials to use during collection analysis. He or she needs tools—such as Quick View Plus, Treesize Pro, and Disk Analyzer—that allow previewing and/or copying digital records and manuscripts without changing the accompanying metadata. An archivist can use these tools to visually inspect the contents of a disk by file formats, dates last modified, and other properties, or to locate duplicate copies of the same files, facilitating appraisal decisions and the development of processing plans.

Gathering Contextual Information

The second task in the archival processing business process is gathering contextual information about the records and manuscripts. The information gathered allows an archivist to adequately describe the materials he or she is working with, and it allows users to better understand those materials. The following sub-tasks enable the gathering of contextual information:

- conducting background research on the person(s), family(ies), or organization(s) responsible for the creation of the records or manuscripts;
- listing events or activities reflected in the records or manuscripts;

- identifying record-keeping practices revealed by the records or manuscripts; and
- describing the functions and activities that led to the generation of the records or manuscripts.

This task does not materially change when dealing with digital records or manuscripts. However, its relative importance in the process does change. During this task, the archivist gathers important clues for understanding the arrangement of digital records and manuscripts, and he or she should begin gathering this information even before acquiring the digital materials. Archivists are very familiar with research strategies and tools for identifying and recording this type of information. For digital materials, an archivist may need to make increased use of digital reference sources, such as Internet biographies and social media records. As he or she locates each reference, the archivist can incorporate it directly into a biographical or historical note added to an accession or descriptive record.

Performing a Conservation Assessment

The third task in the archival arrangement and description business process is performing a conservation assessment. The information gathered during this task allows archivists to ensure that records and manuscripts are properly cared for and that conservation issues (mold, water damage, data corruption, etc.) are identified and dealt with before they become big problems. The sub-tasks are:

- identifying conservation problems;
- segregating problem materials; and
- planning for mitigation of those problems.

The identification of conservation problems for digital materials is a new challenge for archivists. At the most fundamental level, all files should be scanned for potential viruses or other problems that may affect the stability of the system on which the records will be stored or used. If virus-checking software is installed on the computer, this step will probably be done automatically when the files are placed on the machine; archivists should verify the virus definition files are being updated automatically by the provider of the anti-virus software. In addition, an archivist needs to learn about and become familiar with the signs of bit rot, data loss, and other conservation issues associated with digital materials. Validation tools such as DROID and JHOVE/JHOVE2 can be particularly helpful. As mentioned before, these are tools that allow identification and characterization of the file format in which the digital record or manuscript is recorded. They also allow an archivist to verify that a file is what it purports to be, which helps in establishing the authenticity of the materials. An archivist also needs to become comfortable running checksums and creating hash values using tools like the MD5 Hash Generator.[33] These hash values and checksums are used to verify that stored digital materials have not changed. A checksum generator creates a unique identifier for a file. An archivist can tell whether a file has changed by checking the value generated by the checksum generator. If a file has changed, the checksum will not be the same.

The conservation assessment is often performed concurrently with the next task, intellectual arrangement of the records or manuscripts. When dealing with digital records and manuscripts, it is advisable to perform many of the sub-tasks of the conservation task during accessioning. Segregation of problem materials is another challenge. An archivist needs to become comfortable with extracting digital files from corrupted media, restoring damaged files, and performing virus mitigation. Digital forensics tools can help with these steps, as can the aforementioned validation tools. At the end of the day, planning for mitigation of identified problems is the most important outcome of the conservation assessment task. An archivist needs to develop a plan of action before encountering the problem materials and have the resources necessary to implement that plan as a part of the subsequent processing steps.

Providing an Arrangement Scheme/Intellectual Arrangement

The fourth task in the archival processing business process is intellectual arrangement of the records or manuscripts. There are two sub-tasks:

- determining whether the materials have an original order; and
- identifying the relationships between groups of materials within the collection.

Determining whether digital records and manuscripts have an original order can be a challenging task. It is often difficult to tell if

---

33 More information on the MD5 Hash Generator is available at http://www.md5hashgenerator.com/.

creators are relying on the filing functionality native to the computer system that they are using or if they are consciously creating filing categories and placing documents within those categories. An archivist should gather this information from the creator at the point of acquisition, if possible. In the case of hybrid collections, an archivist may be able to infer the order of the digital records from the order of the physical records. This suggests that in many instances an archivist will find it easier to arrange the analog portions of a hybrid collection before tackling the digital components.

The next step involves identifying the relationships between groups of records within a collection. While this is a fairly straightforward task with physical records and manuscripts, it is a complex activity with digital records and manuscripts—particularly if information about the original order of the records is unavailable. This step is further complicated by the fact that multiple copies of digital documents may be located in multiple filing categories, and it is often difficult to determine the original relationships of the digital documents. However, it is extremely important that the archivist note the relationships he or she can identify. While physical items in a manuscript or archival collection typically have a one-to-one relationship with other items, digital items can, and often do, have many-to-many relationships with other items in the collection.

Arranging the Records

Traditionally, the fifth task in the archival arrangement and description business process is physically arranging the records or manuscripts. The physical arrangement task has five sub-tasks:

- rehousing materials;
- arranging materials into series and subseries;
- identifying preservation needs of the materials;
- identifying the formats found in the records and manuscripts; and
- noting the informational content of the records and manuscripts.

The rehousing materials sub-task needs to be examined in light of digital records and manuscripts. Like physical records and manuscripts, digital records and manuscripts need to be properly stored to facilitate their long-term maintenance. These materials need to be moved to stable digital media and properly stored (this will often occur during the accessioning task). These storage environments can include network servers, external hard drives, and portable media (e.g., M-Discs). Networked servers are highly recommended, and an archivist should consult IT staff in making storage decisions.

The second sub-task is arrangement of the materials into series and subseries. In physical processing this often occurs simultaneously with rehousing. When dealing with digital materials, an archivist has several options. In some cases, it will be best to maintain the original order of the records. In others, he or she may wish to actively create an order for the records that mimics physical filing structures, then carefully move the unchanged digital records into those filing structures. In yet other cases, it may be advisable to use a combination of both strategies. This will require that the archivist be familiar with the repository's technology and the process for preventing digital records and manuscripts from being changed during physical arrangement. As pointed out in the AIMS report cited earlier, there are currently no purpose-built tools for helping archivists physically arrange digital records and manuscripts.[34] The archival community needs to develop and publicize these tools. (In the meantime, Appendix C of this module offers some plausible alternatives.) It is critical that archivists document the steps taken to arrange digital records and manuscripts. This should be done in a processing note.

Next, an archivist should identify the preservation needs of the materials. Archivists need to be familiar with the preservation challenges associated with digital media, and they need to have tools that will help identify digital records and manuscripts that are exhibiting those problems. Tutorials like "Digital Preservation Management: Implementing Short-Term Strategies for Long-Term Solutions" will help archivists identify the preservation challenges of digital materials.[35] They also provide archivists with tools and strategies to begin addressing these challenges.

---

34 AIMS Work Group, *AIMS Born-Digital Collections*, 33–34.
35 "Digital Preservation Management: Implementing Short-Term Strategies for Long-Term Solutions," online tutorial developed for the Digital Preservation Management workshop, developed and maintained by Cornell University Library, 2003–2006; extended and maintained by ICPSR, 2007, http://www.dpworkshop.org/.

The fourth step is identifying the formats found in the digital records and manuscripts. Archivists need to become familiar with tools like DROID and JHOVE2 that can be used to identify and characterize various file formats, and they need to understand the various challenges associated with each format. When performing this step in the process, an archivist must decide whether to save the original file format or transform the digital records or manuscripts into formats that are more easily managed in a preservation environment. He or she might decide to do both and keep the original file format and transform it to a more manageable format that can then be managed over the long term. If files are migrated to another form, it is strongly recommended that the original file format also be preserved, to allow for verification of success or for other conversion actions in the future.

The final sub-task is noting the informational content of the digital records and manuscripts. Archivists are developing strategies and tools for gathering this information in order to be successful in the digital world. They are working with creators to get as much information about the collections up front as possible. Tools such as those mentioned in the accessioning task can be used to analyze the content of the digital records and manuscripts. These include Quick View Plus, Treesize Pro, IrfanView, and Disk Analyzer. Each of these allows the user to view, summarize, or analyze the contents of a disk or a directory, and several of them include useful visualization tools.

Describing the Records

The sixth task is describing the records or manuscripts. In the United States, the sub-tasks of this task are shaped by Describing Archives: A Content Standard (DACS). DACS is the American implementation of the General International Standard Archival Description or ISAD(G). There are eight sub-tasks related to description. They are:

- identifying the appropriate level of description for the materials;
- gathering information needed to identify the materials;
- describing the materials and their arrangement;
- describing the access and use conditions for the materials;
- identifying and gathering administrative information about the materials;

- gathering information about related materials;
- identifying and gathering other useful information; and
- creating access points for the materials.

The description task does not fundamentally change when dealing with digital records and manuscripts. The standards mentioned above (DACS and ISAD[G]) are meant to be format agnostic and apply equally well to digital and physical manuscripts and records. However, neither of these standards cover technical metadata, except in a very general sense, because they allow for the generation of a physical or technical requirements note. Standards such as PREMIS and METS (Metadata Encoding and Transmission Standards) provide the ability to track detailed file-level technical metadata for digital records and manuscripts.[36] Sybil Schaefer and Janet M. Bunde's module, *Standards for Archival Description,* provides a more detailed description of these standards and their applicability to archives. Tools such as the the Duke Data Accessioner and the Curator's Workbench can be used to produce some of this technical metadata in an XML format. Descriptive metadata can be created using a number of different tools, including the Archivists' Toolkit, ICA-AtoM, and Archon,[37] as well as word-processing software, spreadsheets, and XML editors.

Creating Access Tools

The seventh, and final, task in the business process of arranging and describing archives is the creation of access tools that facilitate the discovery and use of the manuscripts or records. These tools are the natural outgrowth of describing the materials. There are two sub-tasks:

- identifying the types of access tools to be created; and
- creating the appropriate access tools.

The first sub-task is identifying the types of access tools to create. An archivist needs to determine whether he or she will create MARC cataloging records, finding aids, or some other access tool. It is likely that with digital records and manuscripts, the archivist will need to provide a combination of access tools. The next step is the

---

36 Information about PREMIS is available at http://www.loc.gov/standards/premis/, and information about METS is available at http://www.loc.gov/standards/mets.
37 Archon and Archivists' Toolkit will be superceded by ArchivesSpace in the near future. See http://www.archivesspace.org/.

actual creation of the appropriate access tool. The archivist can use tools like the Archivists' Toolkit and WorldCat to generate MARC records and finding aids. He or she can also encode information about digital records and manuscripts using Encoded Archival Description (EAD). The archivist needs to use tools like CONTENTdm, Rosetta, and institutional repository platforms such as DSPACE and Fedora to provide access to digital records. Daniel Santamaria's module, *Designing Descriptive and Access Systems*, provides ideas about the types of tools available for this work.

Sample Processing Workflow

Note that the major tasks that constitute archival processing have not changed, but dealing with digital records and manuscripts necessitates significant adjustments regarding the steps taken to accomplish those tasks. Archivists must re-engineer those tasks if they wish to facilitate the effective long-term management of digital records and manuscripts. Although the major tasks of the process are the same, several of the component steps can be shifted. One potential rearrangement is as follows:

- Gathering contextual information about the records
    - conduct background research on the person(s), family(ies), or organization(s) responsible for the creation of the records or manuscripts;
    - identify events or activities reflected in the records or manuscripts;
    - identify record-keeping practices revealed by the records or manuscripts; and
    - identify the functions that led to the generation of the records or manuscripts.
- Accessioning the records
    - create case files to manage information about the accession;
    - take physical and administrative control of the materials;
    - review the content and condition of the materials;
    - perform a conservation assessment (previously a separate major task):
        - identify conservation problems,
        - segregate problem materials, and
        - plan for mitigation of those problems;

- rehouse the materials;
  - identify the formats found in the records and manuscripts;
  - note the information content of the records and manuscripts;
  - gather information needed to identify the materials;
  - identify and gather administrative information about the materials; and
  - identify the arrangement and description priority of the materials.
- Intellectual arrangement of the records
  - determine whether or not the materials have an original order; and
  - identify the relationships between groups of materials within the collection.
- Physical arrangement of the records
  - arrange the materials into series and subseries.
- Description of the records
  - identify the appropriate level of description for the materials;
  - describe the materials and their arrangement;
  - describe the access and use conditions for the materials;
  - gather information about related materials;
  - identify and gather other useful information; and
  - create access points for the materials.
- Creation and implementation of access tools[38]
  - identify the types of access tools to be created;
  - create the appropriate access tools; and
  - load records or metadata into the tools.

This list is but one example of a workflow. Rearrangement of the component parts of archival processing will vary from institution to institution. For example, the conservation assessment has been subsumed into the accessioning task in the preceding example, but it might just as easily be completed before taking custody of the records. A repository's archivists should adjust the overall task sequence in light of existing processes and the capabilities of the tools and services available.

---

[38] More information regarding access options and systems may be found in Daniel A. Santamaria's Module 3, *Designing Descriptive and Access Systems*.

Processing Digital Records and Manuscripts 111

Digital Processing: Practices and Procedures

Now that we've mapped and re-engineered the archival processing business process, let's take a look at how it can be applied to collections containing digital manuscripts and records.

Using the OAIS Reference Model

To begin, we should briefly consider the Open Archival Information System (OAIS) reference model. This model was developed by the Consultative Committee for Space Data Systems to establish a framework for preserving digital information. The OAIS model "identifies and describes the core set of mechanisms with which an OAIS-type archive meets its primary mission of preserving information over the long-term and making it available to the designated community."[39] It is one way that the archival processing business process can be reconceptualized to enable archivists to successfully manage digital records and manuscripts.

The OAIS model (Figure 1) describes the procedures for ingesting, managing, and providing access to digital content. It is built around

Figure 1. Open Archival Information System (OAIS) Model

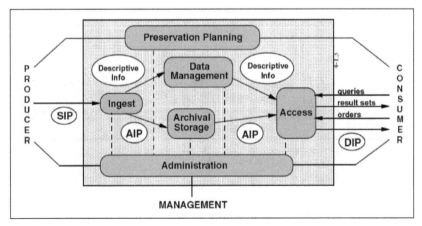

Source: Brian Lavoie, "The Open Archival Information System Reference Model: Introductory Guide," *DPC Technology Watch Report* 04-01 (London: Digital Preservation Coalition, 2004).

---

39 Brian F. Lavoie, "The Open Archival Information System Reference Model: Introductory Guide," *DPC Technology Watch Report 04-01* (London: Digital Preservation Coalition, 2004), accessed December 15, 2012, http://www.dpconline.org/component/docman/doc_download/91-introduction-to-oais.

the concept of information packages. An information package has two components: (1) the digital object and (2) the metadata necessary to support the long-term preservation of that digital object. Understanding two of the information package variants, the submission information package (SIP) and the archival information package (AIP), is a necessary first step toward understanding the impact of digital records and manuscripts on the archival processing business process. The SIP is the "version of the information package that is transferred from the Producer to the OAIS when information is ingested into the archive."[40] It is transferred and generated during the accessioning step of archival processing.

The AIP (Figure 2) is the "version of the information package that is stored and preserved by the OAIS."[41] The AIP comprises the acquired materials, once they have been processed, plus the enrichment data created through arrangement and description. The enrichment data in the AIP includes descriptive, contextual, and structural metadata that allow for future access of the materials. The SIP and the AIP are useful for helping us remember that the long-term preservation of digital objects involves more than just the object itself: it also involves the

Figure 2. Archival Information Package (AIP)

Content Information		Preservation Description Information	
Content Data Object	Representation Information	Reference	Provenance
		Context	Fixity
Packaging Information			
Descriptive Information			

Source: Brian Lavoie, "The Open Archival Information System Reference Model: Introductory Guide," *DPC Technology Watch Report* 04-01 (London: Digital Preservation Coalition, 2004).

---

40 Ibid., 75.
41 Ibid.

metadata (technical and descriptive) associated with the object. One way to look at archival processing is to consider it to be the process of transforming an SIP into an AIP.

The remainder of this section will examine these transformation actions in more detail and will suggest how specific tools can be used to facilitate them.[42]

Preparing to Process

There are typically two ways that archivists encounter digital manuscripts and records. Currently, the most common way is through hybrid collections. Hybrid collections contain both physical and digital materials, and archives have been gathering these types of collections for more than thirty years. The second way is in digital-only or "born-digital" collections. As we move deeper into the twenty-first century, archivists will have to grapple more frequently with accessions that consist solely of digital manuscripts and records. While the specific steps will vary when dealing with a hybrid or digital-only collection, a repository's workflow must be able to accommodate both types of collections.

Traditionally, archival processing has occurred after materials have been acquired. This has to change in the digital environment. Archivists need to gather information necessary for successfully arranging and describing hybrid and digital-only collections from the time that materials are identified, appraised, and selected for acquisition, if not earlier.

Hybrid and digital-only collections present archivists with a host of challenges and opportunities. These challenges and opportunities will require archivists to make adjustments to traditional archival processing. These adjustments are not radical and typically involve adjusting the timing of the tasks that constitute archival processing, as well as using digital tools to undertake actions specific to digital materials. For example, archival processing has traditionally begun after the acquisition of materials. In the new paradigm, these activities need to begin with the decision to acquire materials. This section walks through the processing of digital records and manuscripts.

---

42 In addition to the tools listed below, repositories may wish to evaluate the open-source tool Archivematica, currently under development and available as beta software, for use in the archival processing of born-digital records. It provides for many of the functions listed below, as microservices within a processing application. More information is available at https://www.archivematica.org/.

Digital information is ephemeral. Archivists need to actively identify digital manuscripts and records that they wish to acquire, working cooperatively with creators to ensure that those materials are preserved for the long term. While helping records creators identify which materials are likely to be most valuable, archivists should also identify contextual and descriptive information (metadata) that is associated with those materials. They should determine which formats the repository will accept and develop procedures that will preserve those formats into the future. They can also facilitate the orderly transfer of digital materials to the repository, ensuring that the authenticity of records is preserved. Finally, all of these actions and decisions should be supported by repository policy and documented in accession notes.

Developing Policies and Procedures

Archival processing of hybrid and digital-only collections begins before the decision to acquire materials. Institutions should develop policies to guide their acquisition and stewardship of digital materials: collection development policies that clearly articulate what materials a repository will (and will not) acquire; pre-deposit guidelines that detail the services the repository will provide before digital records and manuscripts are transferred to the institution; transfer guidelines that describe the types of digital records and manuscripts the repository will accept and how those materials will be transferred to the institution; and storage guidelines that detail preservation policies, or how the institution will store digital records and manuscripts, how the institution will manage digital records and manuscripts, and access policies, or how digital records and manuscripts will be made available to patrons.

Once the decision to acquire materials has been made, an archivist needs to communicate with the creator and gather information about the types of digital records and manuscripts that they have. The archivist also needs to begin gathering information about the types of software and hardware used to create the digital files that will be donated. This information will help to inform how the acquired digital materials will be accessioned, arranged, and described. This information should be part of the SIP that is submitted to the archives. The archivist needs to determine what information must be gathered as part of the submission process and then develop procedures specifying how and when that information will be gathered.

As previously mentioned, to successfully accession digital-only records, the repository should have an established policy for how digital content will be captured. This policy should specify how the repository prefers to (1) capture digital media (via direct file copying, creation of disk images, or use of forensics software), (2) treat files after capture has been completed, (3) handle unsuccessful transfers, and (4) acquire accompanying metadata.

Accessioning

Sample Accessioning Workflow

1. Acquire the materials using any of the following methods:
   a. Obtain digital media from the creator. These can include hard drives, compact discs, flash drives, or computers.
   b. Take digital media from the repository to the location of materials and copy them to the digital media.
   c. Transfer files via an FTP server or a utility such as Dropbox.
   d. Use Web capture utilities or e-mail capture tools.
2. Move the acquired materials to a standalone workstation (one not connected to the Internet or institutional network drives).
3. Gather technical metadata.
4. Gather brief descriptive metadata.
5. Survey for formats.
6. Check for personally identifiable information.
7. Scan for viruses.
8. Generate a file manifest, including checksum values.
9. Transfer the files to a production space for arrangement and description.
10. Create copies to use during arrangement and description.
11. Assign a processing priority.
12. Maintain the originals in a secure location.

In most cases, an archivist can either use physical media to capture the digital files or he or she can initiate network- or Web-based transfers or captures. In the case of physical media, the archivist has several options. He or she can take the digital records on media supplied by the creator (hard drives, computers, compact discs, etc.) or provide the media. The archivist can also have files transferred via FTP server or a utility such as Dropbox.

Whatever media is chosen, it is important to view the media as containers of additional materials that form part or all of the collection that has been acquired—materials that will need to be arranged and described. Whatever transfer method is chosen, the archivist needs to become familiar with digital forensics tools and techniques that will enable him or her to successfully transfer the materials without changing them or their associated metadata.[43] Potential tools to use include FTK Imager, Curator's Workbench, the Duke Data Accessioner, Clonezilla, and Thunar; each of these allows bulk file copying and transfer operations and offers the ability to record and test checksums or other values measuring data integrity. If an archivist supplies the transfer media, these tools and techniques will be used onsite. If the archivist is copying files from the media supplied by the donor, receiving materials transferred via FTP, Dropbox, or a similar utility, or is using Web capture or e-mail capture tools, digital forensics tools and techniques will be used at their repository. Network- or Web-based transfers should be carefully managed and the repository should provide a simple way for the donor to provide as much metadata as possible at the time that the digital manuscripts and records are transferred. Collection- or series-level descriptive metadata can be supplied by the records creator in a transfer form, an e-mail message, or a simple Web form, such as that supplied by Google Forms. Once this descriptive metadata has been received, the archivist should attach it to an accession record, so that it can be easily accessed in later stages of processing.

This is a key point that merits repeating: the archivist must gather the metadata associated with the digital files that he or she is acquiring, regardless of transfer method. This includes not only descriptive metadata but also technical metadata. Technical metadata

---

43 Digital forensics projects include The Forensic Investigation of Digital Objects at Kings College London (http://fido.cerch.kcl.ac.uk) and BitCurator Project, sponsored by the University of North Carolina, Chapel Hill, and the Maryland Institute for Technology in the Humanities (http://www.bitcurator.net/).

can be gathered at the time of accession, using tools like the Duke Data Accessioner, NARA's File Analyzer, DROID, Karen's Directory Printer, and the FITS toolset. Ideally, the archivist will create a manifest for the files and folders that include the checksum, date last modified, date created, and folder structure. The archivist should do this at the point of physical transfer while he or she still has relatively easy access to the donor and can quiz the donor about the software and hardware used to create the digital files. The archivist should then bundle the descriptive and technical metadata with the digital files to create a submission information package (SIP). One possible configuration for a SIP is shown in Figure 3.

Once the materials have been transferred to the repository, the archivist needs to briefly examine them to flesh out the description obtained from the donor and to determine if there are any glaring preservation issues that need to be addressed immediately. Ideally, the digital materials will need to be moved from the transfer media to a quarantined workstation (one not connected to institutional networks or the Internet) where an archivist can evaluate them. Following evaluation, the digital materials will be moved to a production space (ideally, this is a dedicated processing workstation, but a segregated network share is also acceptable). While the digital records and manuscripts are on the quarantined workstation, the archivist should generate checksums or hash values using tools like the MD5 Hash

Figure 3. Sample Submission Information Package Structure

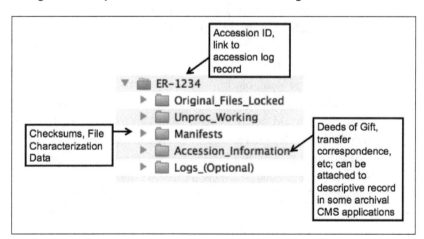

Generator to ensure the integrity of the digital files. The checksums generated at this point will be useful in protecting the authenticity of the digital files over time. They will enable the archivist to detect problems with the files, because the checksum value will change if the file changes. As part of this process, the archivist should perform a virus and malware check on the materials using tools like Symantec, AVG, and McAfee.[44] This important step allows the archivist to identify viruses and malware, then quarantine them before they can infect the computer or a patron's computer. Obsolete or unknown file formats should be identified as part of the transfer for future migration or normalization. Personally identifiable information (e.g., social security numbers, credit card accounts, bank accounts, etc.) needs to be noted, if possible, and restrictions need to be established, if necessary. An important part of accessioning digital records or manuscripts is the creation of an audit trail describing the actions taken on the materials. Tools such as the Duke Data Accessioner (see Figure 4) can be used as part of this process.[45] The archivist should extract as much metadata as possible from the files, in accordance with local policies.

Once the archivist has verified that the digital records and manuscripts are safe, he or she can transfer them to a production space for further descriptive work. At this point the archivist should make copies of the digital files and do any further work on the copies, with the originals retained in a read-only state. After completing these steps, the archivist should quickly review the content of the digital files to flesh out the collection description. With digital manuscripts or records, archivists need to determine the best time for implementing these steps. They can be done as part of the accessioning process or they can be done during arrangement and description. A variety of factors will influence that decision. Important factors to consider include the resources available and donor requirements. The sooner the digital materials are moved off of the carrier media, the better.

Accessioning should occur as soon as possible after selection and acquisition. This enables the repository to ensure the preservation and integrity of the digital content that has been acquired. It also provides

---

44 More information about Symantec is available at http://www.symantec.com/index.jsp. More information about AVG is available at http://free.avg.com/us-en/free-antivirus-download. More information on McAfee is available at http://www.mcafee.com/us/.

45 Information about the Duke Data Accessioner is available at http://library.duke.edu/uarchives/about/tools/data-accessioner.html.

Processing Digital Records and Manuscripts 119

Figure 4. Screen Shot from Duke Data Accessioner

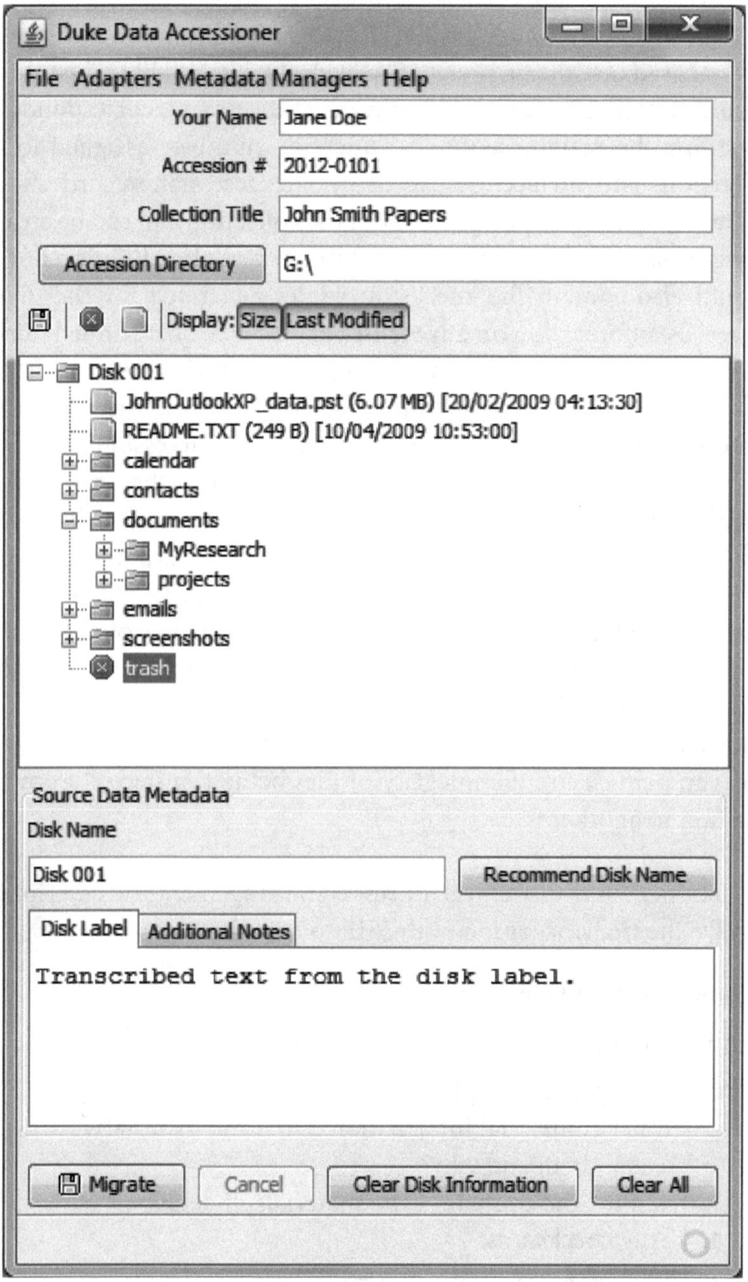

the repository with the option of going back to the creator if something goes wrong during the transfer process.

The archivist should compile all gathered information into either a paper-based case file or, preferably, an electronic case file. The case file should contain the deed of gift or transfer document, correspondence regarding the materials, any identification numbers assigned to the collection, and an accession record. The accession record should contain summary information about the collection and can be created using tools such as the Archivists' Toolkit, ICA-AtoM, or Archon. It should also contain the checksum values generated for the digital materials, information on any viruses or malware quarantined during accessioning, and technical metadata associated with the materials.

Finally, the archivist should assign a processing priority to the materials. In some cases the work done during accessioning will be sufficient to provide access to the materials. In other cases, more detailed arrangement and descriptive work will need to be done.

The archivist will use the information gathered during accessioning to create the SIP referred to in the OAIS model. It consists of the technical and descriptive metadata about the digital object as well as the digital object itself. It also includes the identifier assigned to the materials and the manifest created during accessioning. This information can be bundled together using software like Bagger, a tool that can help ensure the integrity of files being transferred from one location to another.[46]

The next steps of archival processing, arrangement and description, involve the transformation of the SIP to an AIP.

Arrangement and Description

Sample Arrangement and Description Workflow

1. Create processing plan.
2. Gather contextual information about the materials—who created them and why?
3. Examine the content of the materials in detail.
4. Verify checksums.

---

[46] For more information about Bagger, along with a selected list of tools and services of potentially broad interest within the digital preservation community, see http://www.digitalpreservation.gov/tools/.

5. Arrange the materials intellectually (in the case of hybrid collections, use the arrangement of the physical materials to help make arrangement decisions for the digital materials).
6. Arrange the materials physically (if necessary).
7. Describe the materials using EAD, Archivists' Toolkit, Archon, ICA-AtoM, or some other tool.
8. Create access copies.
9. Provide links to digital content.
10. Move materials into a preservation environment.

Once the archivist has completed accessioning the materials, he or she is ready to begin arrangement and description. This process involves transforming the SIP to an AIP. Arrangement and description involve gathering contextual information about the materials, identifying conservation issues, generating technical metadata, arranging the materials, describing them, and creating access tools to help researchers to find and use the records.

Gathering contextual information about the records and manuscripts sets the stage for arranging and describing those records and manuscripts. Understanding who created the materials and why they created them helps the archivist arrange and describe the materials. It aids in the identification of series and subseries. The same holds true for understanding the record-keeping practices that generated the materials. The context of the records and manuscripts is especially important for hybrid collections because it enables archivists to determine the relationships between the physical and digital materials. This allows the archivist to accurately reflect those relationships in the way that the collection is arranged and described. Contextual information can be gathered through discussions with the creator, through transfer documents, and by examining the digital records and manuscripts using tools such IrfanView, Quick View Plus, or Treesize Pro. Much of this information should have been gathered during accessioning and will be available in the collection case file.

The next two arrangement and description tasks typically occur simultaneously. They are performing a conservation assessment and intellectually arranging the materials. If the archivist postponed the transfer of digital files from the carrier media during accessioning, he or she must perform the transfer now, using the concepts and tools described above.

The conservation assessment for digital materials involves the virus and malware check described above as well as monitoring of the checksums created for the digital files. This is a fundamental requirement in ensuring the authenticity of digital documents, because it guards against inadvertent or deliberate changes to the files, thus making it much easier for users to judge authenticity. If the checksums change, that indicates that the digital file has changed. Checksum values should remain the same over time; if they do not, the file has been modified or corrupted in some way on the bit level (the 1s and 0s a computer uses to encode a file).[47] Hybrid collections will also involve a conservation assessment of the physical materials in the collection. The conservation assessment for physical materials involves physically reviewing the materials for signs of mold, water damage, or other potential problems. Once an archivist has identified problem digital or physical materials, he or she must segregate those materials from the rest of the collection and create plans for addressing the problems. The archivist should be looking for conservation problems while examining the manuscripts and records to determine how they should be arranged.

Intellectual arrangement involves: (1) identifying an original order, or lack of order, for the physical and digital material in hybrid collections and for digital material in digital-only collections, and (2) characterizing relationships among items or groups of items.[48] For hybrid collections, it also involves determining the relationships between digital and physical materials and how those relationships will be represented (most likely through the descriptive record created for the collection).

Dealing with digital materials introduces another important component to intellectual arrangement—determining the tools necessary to arrange the digital materials and whether or not the digital materials need to be transformed or migrated to other formats

---

47 Carol Kussman has provided a helpful review of checksum verification tools at http://e-records.chrisprom.com/checksum-verification-tools/.

48 The term *intellectual arrangement* is introduced by the AIMS project partners as a way to indicate that when digital records are arranged, no physical manipulation of the records is necessary. Instead, the main task of arrangement consists of recording appropriate metadata or system pointers to preserve or make clear the relationships of items or groups of items (for example, folders) to one another. University of Hull et al., *AIMS Born-Digital Collections: An Inter-Institutional Model for Stewardship* (January 2012), 43, accessed October 20, 2012, http://www2.lib.virginia.edu/aims/whitepaper/AIMS_final.pdf.

so that they will be usable by researchers. An additional consideration during intellectual arrangement is determining the level at which the collection will be arranged. Will the archivist be creating a collection-level record? Will the collection be divided into multiple series? Will the archivist be describing files or items? The answers to these questions will dictate the types of tools used when dealing with digital materials. The archivist also needs to decide how to integrate digital manuscripts and records into hybrid collections. Will descriptions of the digital records and manuscripts be integrated with the descriptions of the physical records and manuscripts? Or will the digital records and manuscripts form their own series separate from the physical records and manuscripts? While there are no tools specific to the archives community for arrangement work, digital forensics tools can be adapted for this purpose.[49]

Note that arrangement work with digital-only collections is largely intellectual in nature. It involves identifying the relationships between the various components of the digital-only collections. The amount of physical rearrangement of digital materials will vary collection by collection depending on how organized the materials are when received. Even if files or folders are physically rearranged using file management tools, the only change that takes place at a bit level is in the file allocation table or other database that tracks file relationships. (For this reason, it is important to retain a copy of the files as originally accessioned, in a disk image or SIP.) It is often sufficient to leave files in their original arrangement and record descriptive information about the series-level arrangement while completing descriptive work. All arrangement decisions should be fully documented in the descriptive records created by the archivist. The arrangement can be described in tools such as the Archivists' Toolkit, Archon, or ICA-AtoM. The description should clearly identify the connections between the different components of the digital-only collection and, if possible, provide links to the actual digital content. Description should reflect the level of arrangement determined by the archivist and should follow accepted archival descriptive standards.

---

49 Matthew G. Kirschenbaum, Richard Ovenden, and Gabriela Redwine, with research assistance from Rachel Donahue, *Digital Forensics and Born-Digital Content in Cultural Heritage Collections* (Washington, DC: Council on Library and Information Resources, December 2010), accessed July 17, 2012, http://www.clir.org/pubs/reports/pub149/reports/pub149/pub149.pdf. See also the BitCurator Project website at http://www.bitcurator.net/.

Once the archivist has determined the intellectual arrangement, he or she needs to arrange the collection physically. He or she should follow accepted archival practice for the arrangement of physical materials. For hybrid collections, the arrangement of the physical collection provides important clues as to the arrangement of the digital materials. The archivist needs to have a clear understanding of how the creator used the materials, if possible. If the creator relied on search functionality native to his or her computing system, then the archivist should not change how the digital files are related to each other. In this case, the archivist should have two copies of the files with two different arrangements—the original arrangement that is preserved in a dark archive—a holding area for digital files not immediately accessible to end users—and an imposed arrangement that is publicly available and will allow patrons to access the materials. If the creator had a filing system, then the digital materials should be moved into appropriate series and subseries. As the archivist is arranging the materials, he or she should note any preservation problems. For digital materials, it is important to note the different file formats in the collections.

Once the records have been arranged, they need to be described at the level in which they have been arranged. For aggregates (collection, series, subseries, file), DACS is the appropriate descriptive standard. For the description of individual items within a collection, Resource Description and Access (RDA) can also guide descriptive work.[50] An important part of description for hybrid collections will be describing the technical requirements for accessing the digital materials in the collections. Standards like PREMIS and METS can be used to record and share technical metadata.[51] Descriptive work can be completed in tools such as ICA-AtoM, the Archivists' Toolkit, and Archon.

The descriptive work done during arrangement and description should be leveraged as the digital files are moved into a preservation environment. The archivist needs to store and manage both a preservation copy of the digital files (which will be under strict access controls and which will be used only in emergency purposes) and an access copy (which will be used for routine access by archivists and end users). Under normal circumstances, the preservation copy should

---

50 For a concise description, see Karen Coyle and Diane Hillman, "Resource Description and Access (RDA): Cataloging Rules for the 21st Century," *D-Lib Magazine* 13, no. 1 (January/February 2007), http://www.dlib.org/dlib/january07/coyle/01coyle.html.
51 The Library of Congress maintains extensive resource sites for PREMIS and METS at http://www.loc.gov/standards/premis/ and http://www.loc.gov/standards/mets/.

not be accessed but should be stored in a stable environment, such as a replicated file storage infrastructure. The access copy might reside on a Web server or in a nearline environment, where an archivist can quickly retrieve it in response to a user request.

Once descriptions have been created, they need to be made publically available so that the collections are discoverable. This can be done using library catalogs, finding aids, websites/interfaces, and digital collection tools. Linking digital files to their descriptions will greatly improve their discoverability, access, and context.

Appendix A provides two examples of how institutions are processing born-digital records.

Recommendations

Archivists of all stripes (lone arrangers, corporate archivists, government archivists, institutional archivists, manuscripts curators, etc.) can take concrete steps to become more comfortable working with digital manuscripts and records and to arrange and describe hybrid and digital-only collections:

- *Engage with the literature on working with digital materials.* Appendix E provides a list of articles, books, websites, and manuals that illuminate the issues surrounding digital materials. Many of these resources present case studies offering cogent advice on how to implement a program for managing digital manuscripts and records. They offer practical suggestions on how to take existing archival skills and use them to manage digital records and manuscripts, as do the descriptions of recent and current activities in Appendix B.
- *Embrace the concept of digital curation.* Successfully meeting the challenges posed by digital records and manuscripts means that we need to rethink our current archival processing practices. We cannot wait for materials to arrive at our repositories. We must proactively engage with the creators of digital manuscripts and records to ensure that appropriate information is being captured before and during accession. This applies both to organizational records and to personal and family collections.

At the most basic level, we can create a list of questions to ask donors regarding their digital record-keeping practices. Gathering this information will allow us to accurately describe the materials so that they are discoverable, while also permitting us to take the appropriate steps to preserve the materials into the future. We need to develop tools that allow us to add value to the digital records and manuscripts that we are acquiring.

- *Implement a storage solution for existing digital materials.* Don't let the perfect be the enemy of the possible. Look for short-term solutions that can help bridge the gap between current practice and a long-term solution. Ben Goldman states that "for some institutions simple network file storage might be a better start; for others, local file storage on external media might be an adequate short-term solution until more resources are available."[52] Fedora, DSpace, and Rosetta are open-source and commercial software packages designed to help preserve digital content for the long term. These storage solutions are expensive propositions that many institutions will not be able to implement immediately. However, there are relatively inexpensive options available. One of the most intriguing is the M-Disc offered by Millenniata.[53] The M-Disc is described as a permanent file backup disc. Data is stored on the M-Disc by a process that physically alters the recording layer and creates permanent voids or holes. M-Discs are readable on any DVD player. Remember, though, that it is important to make and keep at least two copies of digital manuscripts and records.

- *Develop policies for managing the digital materials that your repository has or will acquire.* Identify the types of digital manuscripts and records that your institution has the capacity to manage. Also identify the types of hardware that can be used to transfer digital manuscripts and records to your repository. Identify the software and formats that you are willing to manage into the future. Establish a baseline for arrangement and description of these materials. Also determine how you

---

52 Ben Goldman, "Bridging the Gap: Taking Practical Steps Toward Managing Born-Digital Collections in Manuscript Repositories," *RBM: A Journal of Rare Books, Manuscripts, and Cultural Heritage* 12, no. 1 (March 2011): 17.

53 More information on the M-Disc is available at http://millenniata.com/.

will handle hybrid collections. These policies will help you successfully manage the digital records and manuscripts that you acquire.
- *Develop a preservation plan.* Start to outline what you hope to accomplish and how you intend to accomplish it. Create a long-term vision for electronic records preservation and then establish short-term goals that will help you to reach your goal. The following questions will help you develop your preservation plan:
  - What is the purpose of your institution? How does preservation of digital manuscripts and records fit in?
  - Will you be OAIS- or TDR- (Trusted Digital Repository) compliant? Partly compliant?
  - What is your mandate?
  - What are the objectives of your digital preservation program?
  - What is the scope of your program?
  - What are your operating principles?
  - What are the roles and responsibilities of members of your organization?
  - What is your collection development policy?
  - Who has access to your materials?
  - What challenges do you face when it comes to digital preservation?
  - How will your program be funded? Institutionally? By donors?
  - How will the technological components of your program be managed?
  - What about security of digital materials?
- *Become comfortable with the available tools.* Software such as that listed in Appendix C can help you arrange and describe the digital manuscripts and records kept by your repository. These tools include checksum generators and file format checkers. These tools will help you gather the information that you need to ensure the authenticity of the digital materials in your holdings. Download some of the tools described in this module and play with them. See if you are comfortable using them and if they will meet your needs. Look at tools in the following areas:
  - Submission/capture/appraisal
  - File metadata/packaging

- Arrangement
- Description
- Integrated tools
- *Participate in workshops on dealing with digital records and manuscripts.* The courses offered in SAA's Digital Archives Specialist (DAS) curriculum and certificate program are one option, as are continuing education classes and workshops.
- *Become familiar with digital forensics.* All archivists need to become familiar with the concepts of digital forensics and how the tools used in digital forensics can help them preserve the authenticity of digital manuscripts and records. Digital forensics is a branch of forensic science encompassing the recovery and investigation of material found in digital devices. Digital forensics tools include Clonezilla, Treesize Free, and FTK Imager.

By keeping these simple principles in mind, and by using new tools and procedures as they are developed, archivists will be able to address the evolving set of issues posed by new digital formats. All archivists can exercise appropriate stewardship over digital materials, and if the challenges seem great, the opportunities to serve our organizations are even greater!

Appendix A: Case Studies

Duke University: David M. Rubenstein Rare Book & Manuscript Library
by Seth Shaw

The David M. Rubenstein Rare Book & Manuscript Library uses two methods to arrange and describe born-digital records. Using the first method, we note the records' logical arrangement, without changing the folder structure. Using the second method, we copy the files and folders into a new structure mirroring the collection's series structure, while retaining a copy of the files and folders as accessioned.

We employed the first method when a collector made a purely digital addition to the Common Sense Foundation records. This accrual represented a network file store snapshot, with known non-permanent records omitted. After securing the materials in our dedicated file store, we placed a working copy of the files on a computer that is dedicated to processing born-digital material to allow for arrangement and description. We used a variety of tools to review file contents. Quick View Plus (a commercial file viewer application supporting thousands of file formats) is a useful general-purpose tool. To examine specific formats more carefully, we made selective use of plain-text editors, the Microsoft Suite, Adobe Acrobat, Irfan Viewer (images), VLC media player (audio/video), and hex-viewers. Each top-level folder was quickly evaluated to identify whether it could be mapped to an existing series or subseries. If a match could not be identified, the second-level folders were analyzed in similar fashion. If second-level review failed, the processing archivist created new series and subseries as appropriate to fit the record content.

In practice, we have found that the processing archivist rarely needs to provide arrangement lower than the second level. Since logical arrangement is used, a folder or subfolder may be listed in multiple series as appropriate. For example, a new "Staff Files" series was created. Sub-folders within two "Staff Files" subseries merited inclusion with the "Board of Directors" series, and so were described there though no files were moved, allowing multiple access points from the finding aid.

When each folder's appropriate arrangement has been identified, it is added to the existing EAD series component element with its own component and container element. The container element's type attribute is "efolder" and label attribute is "Electronic Folder." The container element's text value is the path to the parent folder (if not the top level). The unit title is simply the folder's name. Extent lists folder count, file count, and megabytes (identified on Windows machines by right-clicking and selecting "Properties"). Earliest and latest date modified values are used for date ranges (identified using an in-house script). The scope and content note describe the record content in the same way that analog materials would be described, with additional notes describing common file formats as appropriate.

In some cases, we use an alternate method to arrange and describe the records. The Rubenstein Library's second method allows an archivist to create an electronic series structure (using filesystem directories). Once the series structure has been established, the archivist moves folders and files from their original locations into the appropriate series/directory.

This method was used for the Mark Bowden papers. Note that folders and files are moved only to a single location (and not copied), but may then be cross-referenced in multiple series as described in the previous method. This option is more appropriate when there are several small additions or content spread across multiple media with no artifactual value and is comparable to consolidating papers from several small boxes into a larger one. Associations within the media are not irrevocably lost in this method, because they are preserved in the accessioned structure, though not immediately available to the researcher via the "processed" arrangement.

Brigham Young University Archives:
Sidney B. Sperry Photographs
by J. Gordon Daines III

The following case study illustrates some of the challenges inherent to working with legacy digital-only collections. It highlights simple actions that repositories can take to apply best practices in arranging and describing legacy digital-only collections.

The Sidney B. Sperry photographs were acquired by the Brigham Young University Archives in 2003. Sidney B. Sperry was a faculty member who taught at Brigham Young University from 1932 until 1971. The Sperry photographs collection consists of ten compact discs containing digital scans of photographs of Sidney B. Sperry. The images were gathered from Sperry's descendants for use in a family project. The responsible family member felt that the materials would be of use to a wider community and donated the digital images to the Brigham Young University Archives.

The compact discs contained several hundred TIF images with no discernible organization. The donor provided a spreadsheet listing the file names and a brief description for each of the images. After the discs were accessioned, a virus check was completed to make sure that the files were not infected with a virus or other malware. Each image was viewed and checksums were generated for each file.

Initial review revealed no problems with either the files or the discs, and they were described at a collection level in our library's catalog. The disks were then placed in the L. Tom Perry Special Collections cold vault. They were retrieved from the cold vault periodically and checked to ensure that the images were not deteriorating. This was done by comparing the checksums generated at acquisition of the materials with the checksums generated when the files were reexamined.

When it was discovered that images on one of the discs were failing, the entire collection was copied to new media. In 2010 a networked storage space was made available for digital preservation. The digital files were moved from the compact discs to network storage and were again checked for any problems associated with the files. None were found. In 2012 the Harold B. Lee Library acquired Ex Libris's Rosetta, a digital preservation system. In mid-2012 the archivist began importing the digital files into the library's pilot installation of Rosetta. As part of the import process, a validation stack was run against the digital files to determine if the files were the formats that they purported to be and to verify the checksums. Using Rosetta, additional descriptive metadata was added to the files and they were packaged as an AIP for long-term preservation.

Appendix B: Recent and Current Activities

A number of projects have examined or are examining how to best manage digital-only and hybrid collections. These projects are beginning to produce a body of knowledge that will enable archivists to successfully take responsibility for the digital materials entrusted to their care.

1. Born-Digital Special Collections project: The Born-Digital Special Collections project is an OCLC research initiative that aims to enhance the effective management of the born-digital materials held by special collections repositories. The project aims to create a series of brief reports outlining the skills necessary to manage digital content and a list of tools that archivists can use. Information about the project is available at http://www.oclc.org/research/activities/bordigital/default.htm.

2. Paradigm Project: The Paradigm Project, or Personal Archives in Digital Media, was a research partnership and project between the University of Oxford and the University of Manchester. It explored the problems and challenges involved with preserving personal digital papers. The project staff acquired digital materials from working politicians in the United Kingdom and ran the materials through the archival business process. They created a workbook with best practice guidelines on how to manage digital papers. Information about the project is available at http://www.paradigm.ac.uk/index.html.

3. futureArch: futureArch is a research project out of the Bodleian Library in the United Kingdom. It builds on the work of the Paradigm Project and is a Mellon-funded initiative that is designed to move the curation of born-digital archives and manuscripts from a series of small projects to a sustainable activity integrated with other aspects of the Bodleian Library's operations. Information about the project is available at http://futurearchives.blogspot.com/.

4. Digital Lives Project: This is another research project out of the United Kingdom. It was funded by the Arts and Humanities Research Council and involved team members from the

British Library, University College London, and the University of Bristol. The Digital Lives project brought together experts in digital preservation, digital manuscripts, literary collections, Web archiving, history of science, and oral history to consider personal digital archives and how they will impact research repositories. The Digital Lives project produced a thoughtful workbook (available at http://britishlibrary.typepad.co.uk/files/digital-lives-synthesis02-1.pdf) on the issues surrounding personal digital archives. More information about the project is available at http://www.bl.uk/digital-lives/index.html.

5. DigCCur: DigCCurr (Digital Curation Curriculum) is a project out of the University of North Carolina aimed at creating a graduate-level curricular framework to prepare students to work with digital and data repositories. More information is available at http://ils.unc.edu/digccurr/aboutI.html.

6. Digital POWRR: Digital POWRR (Preserving Objects with Restricted Resources) is investigating, evaluating, and recommending digital preservation solutions that are appropriate for libraries with smaller amounts of data and/or fewer resources. The project is also examining potential business models that would provide equitable access to digital preservation tools in libraries of all sizes. The Northern Illinois University Libraries are leading this research, with partner repositories in Illinois and a nationally representative board of advisors. More information is available at http://digitalpowrr.niu.edu/.

7. Digital Curation Centre: The Digital Curation Centre is the United Kingdom's hub of expertise in curating digital research data. The site provides access to information about digital curation and tools available to those responsible for managing digital content. More information is available at http://www.dcc.ac.uk/.

8. InterPARES 3: The InterPARES (International Research on Permanent Authentic Records in Electronic Systems) project is aimed at developing a knowledge base that will enable the long-term preservation of authentic records that are created and/or stored in digital form. The project, which is currently

on phase 3, is focusing on putting theory into practice. More information is available at http://www.interpares.org/.

9. AIMS Born-Digital Collections: An Inter-Institutional Model for Stewardship: The AIMS project is a partnership between the University of Virginia Library, Stanford University, the University of Hull, and Yale University aimed at creating a scalable framework for stewarding digital-only content. The project team produced a report in January 2012 that contains their recommendations (available at http://www2.lib.virginia.edu/aims/whitepaper/). Information about the project is available at http://www2.lib.virginia.edu/aims/.

10. Practical E-Records: This blog (http://e-records.chrisprom.com/), maintained by Christopher J. Prom at the University of Illinois, Urbana-Champaign, contains useful information about how to begin working with digital content. The blog is the result of a project aimed at evaluating software and conceptual models that archivists can use to identify, preserve, and provide access to digital records.

11. Practical Tools for Electronic Records Management and Preservation: This white paper (http://www.ctg.albany.edu/publications/guides/practical_tools_for_ermp/practical_tools_for_ermp.pdf) is the result of a partnership between the New York State Archives and Records Administration and the Center for Technology in Government that was funded by the National Historical Publications and Records Commission. It discusses the results of their "Models for Action: Practical Approaches to Electronic Records Management and Preservation" project. While a little outdated, this report presents useful information on the management of electronic records.

12. Digital Curation Google Group: This is a public forum designed to provide a space for discussion of the various institutional and consortial efforts, software projects, and standardization initiatives involving digital curation. Information about the group is available at https://groups/google.com/forum/#!forum/digital-curation.

13. Archivematica: Archivematica is an open-source digital preservation system that is designed to maintain standards-based, long-term access to collections of digital objects. It facilitates the use of PREMIS, Dublin Core, METS, and other best practice standards to preserve digital materials. Information about the project is available at https://www.archivematica.org/wiki/Main_Page.

14. Spartan Archive project: The Spartan Archive project is dedicated to developing an electronic records archive for Michigan State University's born-digital records and publications. The project is funded by the National Historical Publications and Records Commission. Information about the project is available at http://www.archives.msu.edu/about/spartan_archive.php.

Appendix C: Selected Tools for Use in Processing Digital Records and Manuscripts

	Transfer/Copy	Secure legal custody	Gather contextual information	Identify conservation issues	Stabilize records	Identify formats, extent, structure	Record checksums	Arrange	Achieve intellectual control
Archivematica https://www.archivematica.org/wiki/Main_Page			X	X	X	X	X		X
ArchivesSpace http://www.archivesspace.org			X						X
Archivists' Toolkit http://www.archiviststoolkit.org/			X						X
Archon http://www.archon.org/			X						X
AVG http://www.avg.com/us-en/homepage						X			
BagIt http://www.digitalpreservation.gov/tools/#b	X	X					X		
Checksums for Windows http://sourceforge.net/projects/checksumwindows							X		
Curator's Workbench http://www.lib.unc.edu/blogs/cdr/index.php/about-the-curators-workbench/	X	X				X	X		X
DROID http://www.nationalarchives.gov.uk/information-management/our-services/dc-file-profiling-tool.htm						X		X	
Duke Data Accessioner http://library.duke.edu/uarchives/about/tools/data-accessioner.html	X			X		X	X		
EADitor http://code.google.com/p/eaditor/			X						X

138   ARCHIVAL ARRANGEMENT AND DESCRIPTION

	Transfer/Copy	Secure legal custody	Gather contextual information	Identify conservation issues	Stabilize records	Identify formats, extent, structure	Record checksums	Arrange	Achieve intellectual control
ExactFile http://www.exactfile.com							X		
FastSum http://www.fastsum.com/							X		
File Checksum Integrity Verifier Utility http://support.microsoft.com/kb/841290							X		
FITS Toolset http://code.google.com/p.fits				X			X	X	
FTK Access Imager http://accessdata.com/products/computer-forensics/ftk	X						X	X	
HashMyFiles http://www.nirsoft.net/utils/hash_my_files.html							X		
ICA-AtoM https://www.ica-atom.org/			X						X
IrfanView http://www.irfanview.com								X	
JHOVE/JHOVE2 http://www.digitalpreservation.gov/partners/jhove2.html						X			
Karen's Directory Printer http://www.karenware.com/powertools/ptdirprn.asp						X	X		
LOC Transfer Tool http://sourceforge.net/projects/loc-xferutils/	X						X		
MD5 & SHA-1 Checksum Utility http://download.cnet.com/MD5-SHA-1-Checksum-Utility/3000-2092_4-10911445.html							X		

Processing Digital Records and Manuscripts 139

Tool	Transfer/Copy	Secure legal custody	Gather contextual information	Identify conservation issues	Stabilize records	Identify formats, extent, structure	Record checksums	Arrange	Achieve intellectual control
MD5 Checker http://download.cnet.com/MD5-Checker/3000-2092_4-10410639.html							X		
NameChanger http://www.mrrsoftware.com/MRRSoftware/NameChanger.html					X			X	
NARA File Analyzer https://github.com/usnationalarchives/File-Analyzer						X	X		
PREMIS in METS Toolbox http://pim.fcla.edu/									X
PRONOM http://www.nationalarchives.gov.uk/PRONOM/Default.aspx						X			
Renamer (Mac only) http://renamer.com/								X	
Renamer by den4b (Windows only) www.den4b.com/?x=products&product=renamer								X	
Statistics New Zealand Prototype PREMIS Creation Tool http://pigpen.lib.uchicago.edu:8888/pigpen/40							X		X
Symantec http://www.symantec.com/index.jsp				X					
Teracopy http://codesector.com/teracopy	X			X					
Thunar http://thunar.xfce.org/								X	
TreeSize http://www.jam-software.com/freeware/								X	
Ultracopier http://ultracopier.first-world.info/	X			X				X	

140 ARCHIVAL ARRANGEMENT AND DESCRIPTION

	Transfer/Copy	Secure legal custody	Gather contextual information	Identify conservation issues	Stabilize records	Identify formats, extent, structure	Record checksums	Arrange	Achieve intellectual control
Unified Digital File Registry http://www.udfr.org								X	
Word Processors					X				X
XML Editors									X

Appendix D: Standards Applicable to the Description of Digital Records and Manuscripts

Standards	Technical Metadata	Descriptive Metadata
DACS (Describing Archives: A Content Standard) http://www.archivists.org/governance/standards/dacs.asp		X
EAC-CPF (Encoded Archival Context—Corporate Bodies, Persons, and Families) http://eac.staatsbibliothek-berlin.de/		X
EAD (Encoded Archival Description) http://www.loc.gov/ead		X
METS (Metadata Encoding and Transmission Standard) http://www.loc.gov/standards/mets/	X	
PREMIS (Preservation Metadata: Implementation Strategies) http://www.loc.gov/standards/premis/	X	
RDA (Resource Description and Access) http://www.rdatoolkit.org/	X	X

Appendix E: Further Reading

AIMS Work Group. *AIMS Born-Digital Collections: An Inter-Institutional Model for Stewardship*, 2012. http://www2.lib.virginia.edu/aims/whitepaper/AIMS_final.pdf.

Carroll, Laura, Eriak Farr, Peter Hornsby, and Ben Ranker. "A Comprehensive Approach to Born-Digital Archives." *Archivaria* 72 (Fall 2011): 61–92.

Cunningham, Adrian. "Digital Curation/Digital Archiving: A View from the National Archives of Australia." *American Archivist* 71 (Fall/Winter 2008): 530–543.

———. "Ghosts in the Machine: Towards a Principles-Based Approach to Making and Keeping Digital Personal Records," in *I, Digital: Personal Collections in the Digital Era*, ed. Christopher A. Lee, 78–89. Chicago: Society of American Archivists, 2011.

Dollar, Charles M. *Authentic Electronic Records: Strategies for Long-Term Access.* Chicago: Cohassett Associates, 2000.

Dow, Elizabeth H. *Electronic Records in the Manuscript Repository.* Lanham, MD: Scarecrow Press, 2009.

Forstrum, Michael. "Managing Electronic Records in Manuscript Collections: A Case Study from the Beinecke Rare Book and Manuscript Library." *American Archivist* 72 (Fall/Winter 2009): 460–477.

Goldman, Ben. "Bridging the Gap: Taking Practical Steps Toward Managing Born-Digital Collections in Manuscript Repositories." *RBM: A Journal of Rare Books, Manuscripts, and Cultural Heritage* 12, no. 1 (March 2011): 11–24.

Greene, Mark A. "MPLP: It's Not Just for Processing Anymore." *American Archivist* 73 (Spring/Summer 2010): 175–203.

Hilton, Chris, and Dave Thompson. "Collecting Born Digital Archives at the Wellcome Library." *Ariadne* 50 (January 2007). http://www.ariadne.ac.uk/issue50/hilton-thompson.

International Council of Archivists. *Electronic Records: A Workbook for Archivists*. April 2005. http://www.wien2004.ica.org/en/node/30273.

John, Jeremy Leighton. "Adapting Existing Technologies for Digitally Archiving Personal Lives: Digital Forensics, Ancestral Computing, and Evolutionary Perspectives and Tools." London: The British Library, 2008. http://www.bl.uk/ipres2008/presentations_day1/09_John.pdf.

John, Jeremy Leighton, with Ian Rowlands, Peter Williams, and Katrina Dean. *Digital Lives: Personal Digital Archives for the 21st Century: An Initial Synthesis*. London: British Library, March 2010. http://britishlibrary.typepad.co.uk/files/digital-lives-synthesis02-1.pdf.

Kirschenbaum, Matthew G., Richard Ovenden, and Gabriela Redwine, with research assistance from Rachel Donahue. "Digital Forensics and Born-Digital Content in Cultural Heritage Collections." Washington, DC: Council on Library and Information Resources, December 2010. http://www.clir.org/pubs/reports/pub149/reports/pub149/pub149.pdf.

Lee, Christopher A., ed. *I, Digital: Personal Collections in the Digital Era*. Chicago: Society of American Archivists, 2011.

Lee, Christopher A., and Helen Tibbo. "Where's the Archivist in Digital Curation? Exploring the Possibilities through a Matrix of Knowledge and Skills." *Archivaria* 72 (Fall 2011): 123–168.

Mas, Sabine, Dominique Maurel, and Inge Alberts. "Applying Faceted Classification to the Personal Organization of Electronic Records: Insights into the User Experience." *Archivaria* 72 (Fall 2011): 29–59.

Peters, Catherine Stollar. "When Not All Papers Are Paper: A Case Study in Digital Archivy." *Provenance* 24 (2006): 23–35.

Williams, Peter, Jeremy Leighton, and Ian Rowland. "The Personal Curation of Digital Objects: A Lifecycle Approach." *Aslib Proceedings: New Information Perspectives* 61, no. 4 (2009): 340–363.

MODULE 3
DESIGNING DESCRIPTIVE AND ACCESS SYSTEMS

Daniel A. Santamaria

Table *of* Contents

Introduction • 148

Pre-custodial and Pre-accessioning Work • 149

Accessioning Archival Materials • 153

Describing Archival Materials • 155
    Creating New Data • 156
        Catalog Records • 156
        Finding Aids • 158
            Encoded Archival Description • 158
            Archival Collection Management Systems • 159
            Locally Developed Databases and Tools • 161
            Webforms • 163
            Text and XML Editors • 163
        Other Descriptive Data and Outputs • 164
            Encoded Archival Context—Corporate Bodies, Persons, and Families (EAC-CPF) • 164
            Digital Object Metadata • 166
    Managing Legacy Data • 167
    Reducing Backlogs and Managing Collections • 170

Delivering Descriptive Data and Providing Patron Access • 172
    EAD Delivery Mechanisms • 172
    Discovery Layers • 176
    Non-EAD Finding Aid Delivery • 177
    Catablogs and Content Management Systems • 177
    Digital Objects/Digitization • 180
    User Contributions : Patron-initiated Digitization, Description, and Crowdsourcing • 182

Evaluating Access Systems and User Services • 186

Conclusion • 189

Appendices
  Appendix A: Summary of Recommendations • 191
  Appendix B: Case Studies
    Princeton University Archives • 193
      by Daniel A. Santamaria
    Shelby White and Leon Levy Archives Center, Institute for
      Advanced Study • 202
      by Christine Di Bella
  Appendix C: Selected Tools Supporting Description and Access • 207
  Appendix D: Further Reading • 208
  Appendix E: Sample Workflow and Tools for Small Repositories • 214

ABOUT THE AUTHOR

Daniel A. Santamaria is assistant university archivist for technical services at the Seeley G. Mudd Manuscript Library at Princeton University, where he oversees all technical services operations, including accessioning, processing, and descriptive practices. He previously worked at the New York Public Library and both the Clements Special Collections Library and the Bentley Historical Library at the University of Michigan. He holds an MSI from the University of Michigan's School of Information and a BA in history from Wesleyan University. He developed and teaches the workshop "Implementing More Product, Less Process" for the Society of American Archivists and is currently working on a book on extensible processing practices for the American Library Association.

Introduction

More than five decades ago, Theodore Schellenberg wrote that "use is the end of all archival effort."[1] Though most twenty-first-century archivists would agree with Schellenberg's sentiment, methods of providing access have changed dramatically over the last two decades. Since the 1980s, archivists have seen the development of new structure and communication standards such as the MARC Format for Archival and Manuscripts Control (MARC AMC) and later Encoded Archival Description (EAD), as well as new content standards such as *Describing Archives: A Content Standard* (DACS) and *General International Standard Archival Description* (ISAD[G]). They have also witnessed the development of now commonly available software and hardware tools that facilitate the production of descriptive information. Perhaps most importantly, archivists have witnessed the development of the World Wide Web, which promises the ability to provide twenty-four-hour universal access to archival material.

Despite these developments, there is evidence that many archival repositories struggle to provide access to their holdings. According to a comprehensive survey of research libraries published in 2010, only 44 percent of archival collections are represented by an online finding aid. Far less material, whether digitized or born digital, is actually available online.[2] Small archival and special collections repositories may struggle even more to provide adequate access to the materials in their care.

In the twenty-first century, archivists have a seemingly endless, sometimes overwhelming number of tools and strategies to use in making their holdings widely available. Whatever the size or staffing level of a repository, archivists can implement tools that will allow them to make both descriptive information and actual archival content more accessible to more users.

This module describes some of those tools, concentrating on those that constitute the major components of an archival descriptive and access system. These tools support pre-accessioning activities, accessioning, description, the delivery of descriptive records and

---

[1] Theodore R. Schellenberg, *Modern Archives: Principles and Techniques* (Chicago: University of Chicago Press, 1956), 224.
[2] Jackie M. Dooley and Katherine Luce, *Taking Our Pulse: The OCLC Research Survey of Special Collections and Archives* (Dublin, OH: OCLC Research, 2010), accessed October 13, 2010, http://www.oclc.org/research/publications/library/2010/2010-11.pdf.

content, and the evaluation of services. For each of these areas, the module provides implementation recommendations, ranging from the simple to the advanced.

As J. Gordon Daines III writes in Trends in Archives Practice Module 2, *Processing Digital Records and Manuscripts*, archival arrangement and description can be viewed as a business process, or a "series of interrelated activities, crossing functional boundaries, with specific inputs and outputs."[3] Archivists who design and implement archival access systems must understand the series of steps and tasks necessary to create descriptive records, deliver those records and associated content to users, and implement an effective and comprehensive access strategy. Figure 1 provides a list of activities related to implementing descriptive and access systems. A variety of tools and services can be used to support each of these processes.

Establishing archival business processes and workflows is a fundamental first step toward designing an access strategy. Many tools and approaches facilitate the production of good descriptive records and provide access to them; other tools and systems allow for the delivery of digital content, collection management activities, and evaluation of access systems and services. This module examines the activities involved with completing descriptive work and building access systems, grouped in sections and subsections corresponding to the activities outlined in Figure 1.

Pre-custodial and Pre-accessioning Work

Many archivists recognize the benefits of working with records creators to help them manage records that may have archival value, even before the records themselves are formally transferred to an archival repository. Pre-custodial intervention provides a number of benefits related to the design and implementation of descriptive and access systems. The creators of archival material frequently possess expert subject knowledge that accessioning and processing archivists lack. Creators also understand the context of the creation of records—the how and why the records have been created and used—and they may

---

3   Colin Armistead and Simon Machin, "Business Process Management: Implications for Productivity in Multi-State Service Networks," *International Journal of Service Industry Management* 9, no. 4 (1998): 324. Quoted in Daines, *Processing Digital Records and Manuscripts*, p. 100, footnote 30.

> **Figure 1. Description and Access Activities**
> - Pre-custodial and pre-accessioning work
> - Accessioning archival materials
> - Describing archival materials
>   - Creating new data: catalog records, finding aids, and other descriptive data
>   - Managing legacy data: structured data, word-processed data, and printed finding aids and lists
>   - Reducing backlogs and managing collections
> - Delivering descriptive records and providing patron access
>   - EAD delivery mechanisms
>   - Discovery layers
>   - Non-EAD finding aid delivery
>   - Catablogs and content management systems
>   - Digitization and digital objects
>   - User contributions: patron-initiated digitization, description, and crowdsourcing
> - Evaluating access systems and user services

be able to communicate this contextual information more efficiently and effectively than an accessioning or processing archivist. In the case of electronic records, the records creators may also possess systems that the archival repository does not, making it much easier for the creator to view and describe files. Given the large volume of twentieth- and twenty-first-century archival collections, archivists also often need to discuss and document information regarding potential access restrictions and privacy issues with records creators.

Archivists have a large number of tools available for working with records creators in order to manage records and capture data. Those archivists who are involved in organizations that benefit from the services of a formal records management program sometimes have access to commercial software packages. Such software ranges from tools designed to manage records through their entire life cycle (such software is typically called Enterprise Records Management Systems) to document management tools. Among other functions, such tools allow for the creation of file plans and the bulk application of metadata to files. Other repositories use homegrown records management solutions. Guidance for selecting records management software from an archival perspective can be found in a number of places, including the websites of state and federal agencies responsible for government records. These agencies include the New York State Archives[4] and National Archives and Records Administration (NARA).[5]

Enterprise-wide records management systems may be beyond the reach, or out of the control, of many archivists and archival institutions. However, there are other tools that archivists can use to capture the descriptive and other data needed to effectively accession, arrange, describe, and provide access to archival materials. At minimum, archivists should make sure that any descriptive information entered into a records management system can be exported in a structured format, such as XML or tab-delimited text files. Once records are exported in these formats, they can be manipulated and imported into the tools used by the repository or they can be converted directly to a standardized format, such as Encoded Archival Description (EAD). For archivists, a productive first step may be requesting an export of data from the records creators. Once data is exported, individual data elements can be mapped to those required for a single-level minimum descriptive record, as prescribed in *Describing Archives: A Content Standard* (DACS).[6]

Archivists working at institutions that lack records management programs or established systems have a number of options available. Some institutions repurpose their collection management systems in order to collect data related to active and non-permanent records. For example, Michigan State University's archival repository developed records management functionality within the Archivists' Toolkit (AT), a tool used primarily for archival description and collection management.[7] The repository used the Archivists' Toolkit to manage

---

4   Nancy Graham Moreland, *Guidelines for Choosing Records Management Software*, Publication No. 63 (Albany: New York State Archives, 2002), accessed October 14, 2012, http://www.archives.nysed.gov/a/records/mr_pub63.pdf.
5   National Archives and Records Administration, "Recommended Practice: Evaluating Commercial Off-the-Shelf (COTS) Electronic Records Management (ERM) Applications," National Archives, November 2005, accessed October 14, 2012, http://www.archives.gov/records-mgmt/policy/cots-eval-guidance.html#method-4.
6   Society of American Archivists, *Describing Archives: A Content Standard* (Chicago: Society of American Archivists, 2007).
7   Rich Burgis, Ed Busch, Cynthia Ghering, and Whitney Miller, "Using Archivists' Toolkit for Records Management," poster presented at the 2011 Society of American Archivists Research Forum, August 23, 2011, accessed October 14, 2012, http://files.archivists.org/researchform/2011/Slides-Handouts-Posters/Busch-ResearchForumPoster11.pdf.

both permanent and non-permanent records by setting up two separate repositories in a single Archivists' Toolkit installation.

Perhaps the most common pre-custodial approach is to ask records creators and donors to complete a webform or spreadsheet. This form or spreadsheet serves as a transfer and inventory form. It allows the archives some control over the type of data that is collected and provides structured data that can be converted to standard archival descriptive formats, either immediately at the time of accession or as time allows. While some repositories find it tempting to rely on paper forms or word-processed documents to track and transfer information about records, these unstructured formats should be avoided, if at all possible. Although word-processed documents are a slight improvement over paper forms, usually the information included in such documents is much more difficult to repurpose because the information is not created in a structured form. "Structured" does not have to mean "complicated"; structured data can be something as basic as a simple spreadsheet created in Microsoft Excel, as shown in Figure 2.

Repositories can use spreadsheets to capture a simple inventory data, but online forms can capture more nuanced and contextual

Figure 2. Princeton University Archives Records Transfer Form

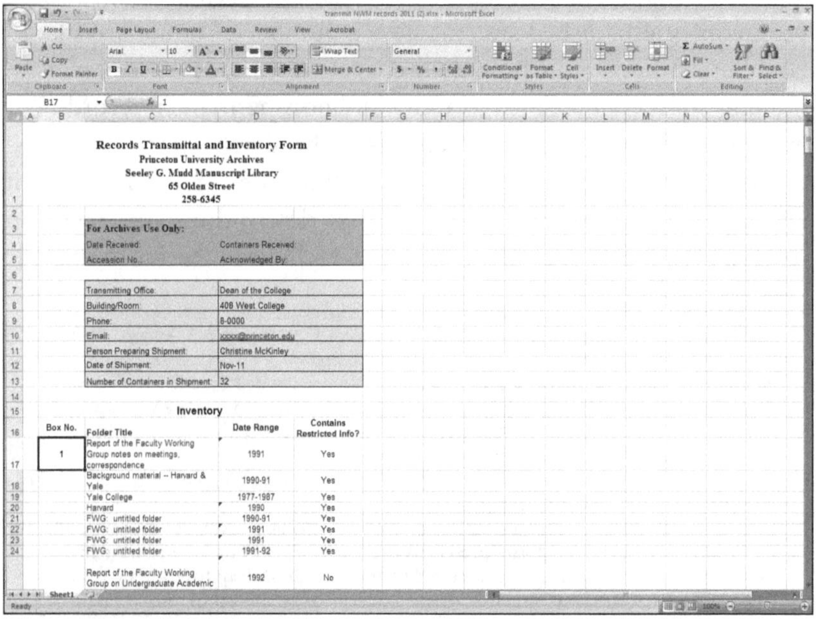

Records Transmittal and Inventory Form
Princeton University Archives
Seeley G. Mudd Manuscript Library
65 Olden Street
258-6345

For Archives Use Only:	
Date Received:	Containers Received:
Accession No.:	Acknowledged By:

Transmitting Office:	Dean of the College
Building/Room:	408 West College
Phone:	8-0000
Email:	xxxx@princeton.edu
Person Preparing Shipment:	Christine McKinley
Date of Shipment:	Nov-11
Number of Containers in Shipment:	32

Inventory

Box No.	Folder Title	Date Range	Contains Restricted Info?
1	Report of the Faculty Working Group notes on meetings, correspondence	1991	Yes
	Background material -- Harvard & Yale	1990-91	Yes
	Yale College	1977-1987	Yes
	Harvard	1990	Yes
	FWG: untitled folder	1990-91	Yes
	FWG: untitled folder	1991	Yes
	FWG: untitled folder	1991	Yes
	FWG: untitled folder	1991-92	Yes
	Report of the Faculty Working Group on Undergraduate Academic	1992	No

information. Simple databases or free online products, including Google Forms, are often used to capture data regarding transfers and donations, such as scope and contents statements, information about the creation and use of the records, and even biographical and historical context related to the records creators.

Accessioning Archival Materials

Accessioning, the act of taking legal and, often, physical custody of archival material, is a necessary early step in preparing archival materials for description and access. Historically, accessioning has often meant recording brief descriptive information about the materials received, as well as administrative information, such as donors' names and addresses. In recent years, due to a growing awareness of the need to reduce backlogs and make descriptive data about holdings available to potential users, archivists have demonstrated increased interest in capturing more descriptive data and in completing enough processing work to make collections available to researchers immediately following accessioning.[8] Individual repositories need to define appropriate baseline levels of description, but ideally each descriptive record created will meet DACS requirements for single-level minimum records, as shown in Figure 3. Larger repositories may also require

Figure 3. DACS: Single-level Minimum Records
- Reference Code Element (DACS Rule 2.1)
- Name and Location of Repository Element (2.2)
- Title Element (2.3)
- Date(s) Element (2.4)
- Extent Element (2.5)
- Name of Creator(s) Element (2.6)
- Scope and Content Element (3.1)
- Conditions Governing Access Element (4.1)
- Language and Scripts of the Material Element (4.5)

---

8   Christine Weideman, "Accessioning as Processing," *American Archivist* 69 (Fall/Winter 2006): 274–283.

some form of multi-level records, which include inventories of boxes or digital files.

An ideal accessioning system will fulfill the dual needs of creating and repurposing both descriptive and administrative data. The ideal accessioning tool will also support the importing of structured data from other sources, such as tab-delimited files, XML files, or other file types.

Several of the most comprehensive accessioning tools also function as collections management systems, including major open-source tools that have been developed over the past five to seven years. For archivists working in the United States, the most prominent of these tools are the Archivists' Toolkit and Archon.[9] A comparison of these two tools is available in Lisa Spiro's 2009 report *Archival Management Software*, created for the Council on Library and Information Resources (CLIR).[10] In general, the Archivists' Toolkit provides a more flexible Accessions module, with more than forty data fields available and functionality to link to documentation such as deeds of gifts and donor correspondence stored outside of the Archivists' Toolkit itself (see Figure 4). While it does not include as many data fields, the Archon accessioning module is still likely to be an effective tool for many small and medium-sized repositories, and it offers the valuable option of publishing accession records directly.

Instead of implementing the Archivists' Tookit and Archon for accessioning, many repositories maintain locally developed accessions databases, often created using Microsoft Access or Filemaker Pro. These databases can be simple or complex in structure. Databases with multiple tables and relationships are often helpful in creating and managing data, but, at minimum, repositories should make sure to map any descriptive data so that it adheres to the DACS requirements for single-level minimum records. Doing so will facilitate the reuse of data and its conversion to EAD, MARC, or other structured formats.

Recording accession information in a simple spreadsheet is one of the simplest ways to create accessions data electronically. The spreadsheet may include columns for descriptive data, location and

---

9 At the time of this writing, Archivists' Toolkit and Archon were merging into a single tool, ArchivesSpace. More information about ArchivesSpace can be found in the section on creating descriptive data.

10 Lisa Spiro, *Archival Management Software: A Report for the Council on Library and Information Resources* (Washington, DC: Council on Library and Information Resources, January 2009), accessed October 14, 2012, http://www.clir.org/pubs/reports/spiro/.

Figure 4. Archivists' Toolkit Accessions Module

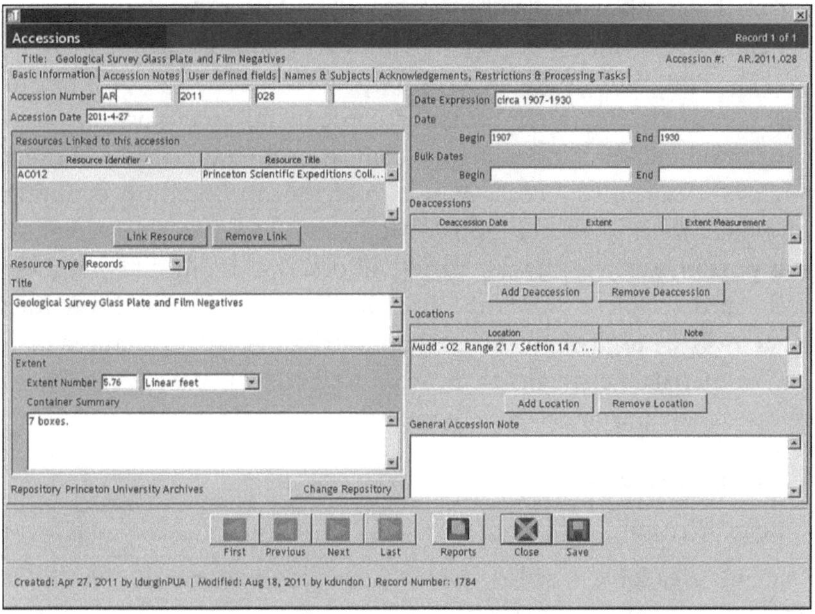

collection management data, and donor information. Though this is not a particularly technologically advanced approach, the data created is keyword searchable, sortable, and extensible because data can be mapped and imported to other systems when resources permit.

Accessioning of born-digital material can and should be executed using principles similar to those applied to paper records, but this task does require some additional procedures and the use of specialized tools. For more information, see Module 2, *Processing Digital Archives and Manuscripts,* in Trends in Archives Practice.

Describing Archival Materials

Description is the key step in any archival workflow or process. The primary purpose of creating descriptive records is to help users discover and make effective use of materials relevant to their research needs.[11] When creating descriptive records, archivists should refer to the four user tasks defined by the library community's *Functional Requirements*

---
11 Wendy Duff and Catherine A. Johnson, "A Virtual Expression of Need: An Analysis of E-Mail Reference Questions," *American Archivist* 54 (Spring/Summer 2001): 43–60.

for Bibliographic Records (FRBR): find; identify, select, and obtain material described in descriptive records.[12] Descriptive records and systems should allow users to perform each of these tasks.

The end result of the descriptive process should also be a record that communicates the information content and functional purposes of archival material, including the context of their creation and use.[13] Archival descriptive records exist in many forms, the most common of which are finding aids and MARC catalog records. Nevertheless, it is possible to create a wide variety of descriptive outputs that meet archival descriptive standards. As noted for accessioning, no matter what tools are used, repositories should strive to create structured data and to map data elements to those prescribed by DACS, ISAD(G), or, in rare cases, another content standard.

Creating New Data

Catalog Records

Machine-Readable Catalog (MARC) records are one of the oldest and most established forms of descriptive records created by archival repositories, dating back as far as the 1970s. Library systems designed to create, manage, and deliver MARC data are among the most stable and commonly available tools available to small archival repositories. Even archivists at many smaller repositories, ranging from those working with small local history collections held within public libraries or local historical societies to archivists in small colleges and universities, likely have access to a MARC-based cataloging system, such as that shown in Figure 5.

Archivists working at repositories without access to these types of systems may be able to partner with other local institutions or work with vendors to set up a system. For example, as of early 2012, OCLC was offering a service which, according to its website, will allow repositories "to quickly and easily set up a website that provides basic

---

12 "Functional Requirements for Bibliographic Records (FRBR) is a conceptual entity-relationship model developed by the International Federation of Library Associations and Institutions (IFLA) that relates user tasks of retrieval and access in online library catalogues and bibliographic databases from a user's perspective." "Functional Requirements for Bibliographic Records," *Wikipedia,* last modified July 17, 2012, accessed October 14, 2012, http://en.wikipedia.org/wiki/Functional_Requirements_for_Bibliographic_Records.

13 Richard Pearce-Moses, *A Glossary of Archival and Records Terminology* (Chicago: Society of American Archivists, 2005), accessed October 13, 2012, http://www2.archivists.org/glossary.

Figure 5. MARC Catalog Record in an Integrated Library System

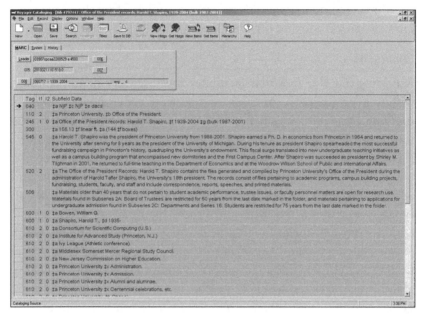

functionality for making small collection information available on the Web, setting up users, checking materials in and out, placing holds, and providing library contact, location, service and event information" through its Websites for Small Libraries project.[14]

In recent years librarians and others have questioned whether the MARC format is a suitable structure for recording descriptive data in the twenty-first century.[15] Many archivists have also challenged the effectiveness of MARC as a structure standard for archival description, because MARC was not designed for that purpose. Given the large number of tools for creating and managing the data, however, as well as the number of tools available to convert MARC data to other formats, creating MARC records remains an option when creating descriptive data for smaller and resource-challenged repositories.

Often archival repositories have access to an Integrated Library System, a tool that bundles functionality for a variety of library

---

14 "OCLC Website for Small Libraries project makes getting on the Web easy and fast for small libraries," Library Technology Guides, February 14, 2012, accessed October 13, 2012, http://www.librarytechnology.org/ltg-displaytext.pl?RC=16561.

15 Karen Calhoun, "The Changing Nature of the Catalog and Its Integration with Other Discovery Tools," report for the Library of Congress, March 17, 2006, accessed October 13, 2012, http://www.loc.gov/catdir/calhoun-report-final.pdf.

functions, such as cataloging, circulation, and acquisitions. For those that do not, comparisons and reviews are available from the American Library Association and other sources.[16]

Finding Aids

A finding aid is a tool that facilitates the discovery of information within a group of records or manuscripts that are related by a unifying characteristic, such as their circumstance of creation or the format of material. Archivists have created finding aids for decades. Finding aids most commonly take the form of a single document that places archival materials in context by consolidating descriptive and administrative information about the collection. This information typically includes acquisition and processing data, provenance data, administrative histories/biographical notes, scope and contents notes, extent statements, and organization and arrangement notes. Many finding aids also include an inventory of components of the collection, at the level of series, sub-series, files, or (less frequently) items. Specific guidance on the elements required for creating minimum, optimum, and value-added finding aids can be found in DACS.

Encoded Archival Description (EAD). EAD is a data structure standard for encoding archival finding aids. Archivists have been encoding finding aids in EAD since the mid-1990s. EAD complements data content standards such as ISAD(G) and DACS. It has been implemented by a wide variety of institutions, not only in the United States and Canada, but also throughout Europe, Australia, New Zealand, and Asia.[17]

EAD is an XML-based standard, and like many standards developed by other cultural heritage professions, it can be mapped to other formats, such as Dublin Core, MODS, MARC, and VRA Core. Despite the many advantages that EAD offers, some repositories have struggled to implement it. Many of the obstacles to creating EAD-encoded data, as well as possible strategies for addressing those obstacles, are discussed by Michele Combs et al. in the OCLC report,

---

16 Anne A. Salter, "Integrated Library System Software for Smaller Libraries," *Library Technology Reports* 39, no. 3 (May/June 2003).

17 Summarized from Michele Combs, Mark A. Matienzo, Merrilee Proffitt, and Lisa Spiro, *Over, Under, Around, and Through: Getting Around Barriers to EAD Implementation* (Dublin, OH: OCLC Research, 2010), accessed October 13, 2012, http://www.oclc.org/research/publications/library/2010/2010-04.pdf.

Over, Under, Around, and Through: Getting Around Barriers to EAD Implementation (2010; hereafter called the *Barriers to EAD* report).[18]

Archival Collection Management Systems. Since approximately 2006, many institutions have adopted collection management tools, such as the Archivists' Toolkit, Archon, and, more recently, ICA-AtoM, to facilitate the creation, management, and display of descriptive data (see Figure 6). When considering options for creating and managing finding aids and other descriptive data, archivists should first investigate these types of tools.

In late 2009, the Andrew W. Mellon Foundation provided funding for a project titled ArchivesSpace, designed to integrate the best features of Archon and the Archivists' Toolkit into a single application. Project partners include the New York University Libraries, University of California, San Diego Libraries, and the University of Illinois, Urbana-Champaign Libraries. According to the project website, the project team is developing a technical platform, governance structure, and service model that will provide the archival community with a cutting-edge,

Figure 6. Archivists' Toolkit Resources Module

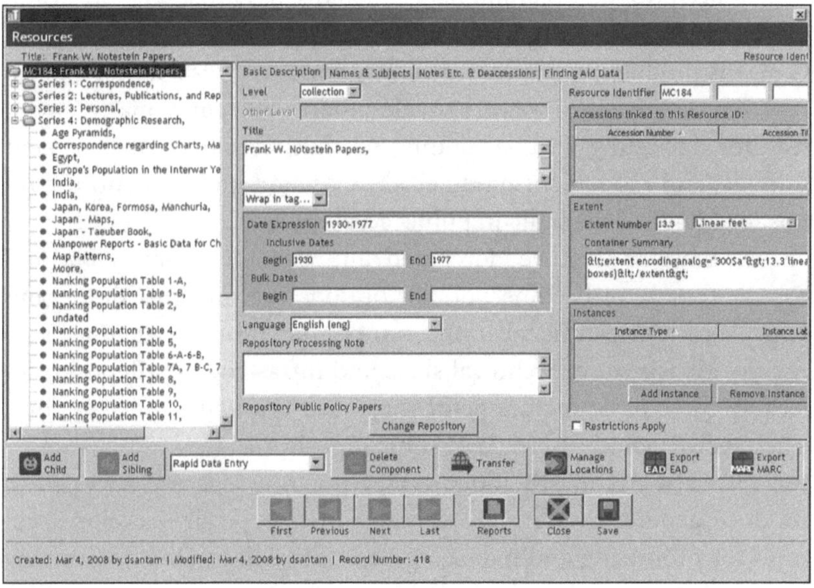

---

18 Ibid.

extensible, and sustainable platform for describing analog and born-digital archival materials.[19]

As with accessioning software, Lisa Spiro's 2009 report on archival collection management tools provides detailed comparisons of several tools for creating descriptive data. The Archivists' Toolkit, Archon, and ICA-AtoM are all based on relational databases. They allow users to create descriptive data by inputting information into fairly simple data entry forms. All allow for the export of archival finding aids as EAD files. Archon and ICA-AtoM also include a public access module, essentially allowing archival repositories to display their descriptive data online with the push of a button. The Archivists' Toolkit does not include a public access function, but, in addition to EAD export, it allows for exporting of HTML and PDF finding aids that repositories can easily post online.

These systems are tremendously powerful tools in creating and managing descriptive data. They allow for efficient data creation and enforce rules for data entry, ensuring that descriptive records conform to standard data structures. All repositories should consider implementing one of these three tools before investigating any other options. In addition to Spiro's report, there are a large number of conference presentations and papers that discuss implementation and use of the Archivists' Toolkit, Archon, and ICA-AtoM (see Appendix C of this module). Generally speaking, most archivists have reported that the Archivists' Toolkit provides more collection management features, including an accessioning module, locations management module, and assessment module, while Archon and ICA-AtoM have the advantage of the built-in public access feature.

As these tools have developed and become more stable and robust, they have become popular options for small, medium, and large repositories. Installation, setup, and routine maintenance require a basic set of technical skills and infrastructure. Repositories lacking these basic requirements may need to pursue other options. The specialized access needs of some repositories may not be met by tools like the Archivist's Toolkit and Archon, which are designed to produce generic output. These repositories typically develop local tools for producing and managing descriptive data. One option may

---

[19] For the latest information about ArchivesSpace, see http://www.archivesspace.org.

be to develop an XSLT stylesheet (or to tailor an existing one, such as those provided by the Online Archives of California) to transform the generic EAD output from a collection management tool to meet the more specific display practices of individual institutions.[20]

Locally Developed Databases and Tools. Some repositories develop relational databases that provide some of the functions of the Archivists' Toolkit and Archon. Staff enter descriptive data into forms and output data as EAD or in other structured formats. Commercially available database software such as Microsoft Access or FileMaker Pro may be used for these purposes and allow for databases with simple or complex structures. Though the goal of every repository's archivists should be to represent their collections online, archivists at the smallest repositories may find this difficult to achieve. Archivists at such repositories may need to maintain their local database solely as an onsite tool for patrons and staff until they can develop methods for delivering descriptive records online.

As with accessioning data, in cases where even the creation of a local database is out of the reach of a smaller repository, archivists can use spreadsheets to create structured descriptive data. Spreadsheets have the advantage of providing an easy data entry method, robust options for sorting and filtering data, and the ability to output data in a variety of formats. As mentioned above, every effort should be made to map descriptive elements to DACS.

Spreadsheets do not provide as much functionality as databases; for example, they do not allow for the establishment of relationships between multiple tables, which often eases data entry and data management. Spreadsheets are well suited, however, to creating inventories or component-level data in EAD, especially for collections with simple arrangement hierarchies. They are less useful for creating collection-level data, which can contain larger chunks of narrative text. When no other tools are available, however, collection-level data can be created in separate tabs in a single spreadsheet or even in multiple spreadsheets.

No matter the size of a repository, it is likely that certain projects and situations will require the use of multiple tools. Nearly all repositories

---

20 Among many other repositories, the Online Archive of California has developed XSLT stylesheets for this purpose. See http://www.cdlib.org/services/dsc/tools/ead_toolkit.html for more information.

receive descriptive data in a variety of formats. Structured data, in the form of spreadsheets, databases, XML, or tab- or other delimited files, is the most useful. This data can typically be mapped and converted to archival descriptive elements. Word-processed or unstructured text files may also be mapped, but unstructured data typically requires extensive manipulation before it can be saved in a more usable structured form. In extreme cases, particularly for repositories with few technical resources, cutting and pasting or even rekeying may allow work to be completed more quickly than attempting to find an automated solution.

Large-scale processing projects may also benefit from solutions outside of the use of collection management software such as the Archivists' Toolkit and Archon. Because both software packages present staff with limited views of the data, they seem well-suited to projects in which physical arrangement has already been determined and data can be entered sequentially. The more advanced sorting and filtering features of an average commercially available or open-source spreadsheet allows users to manipulate data in multiple ways; for example, sorting titles alphabetically, or dates chronologically, often reduces the need to perform physical arrangement or rearrangement during processing.

Often repositories use spreadsheets and databases in conjunction with a more robust collection management system. For example, descriptive information for a "Contents List" or inventory can be created in a spreadsheet. The data in the spreadsheet can then be exported as XML and converted to EAD. Once the data can be validated as EAD, it can be easily imported into the Archivists' Toolkit or Archon or other collection management system for long-term management.

Mapping fields in the spreadsheet to EAD elements is the key step in converting data in a spreadsheet to EAD. The spreadsheet conversion itself can be accomplished in a variety of ways: using the XML export functionality built into the spreadsheet software, converting to XML using a separate process such as a mail merge,[21] or importing directly into an XML editor such as oXygen. North Carolina State University

---

21 A number of repositories have developed methods of converting data to EAD using mail merge functionality. Among them are Yale University's Manuscripts and Archives Department (see http://atatyale.blogspot.com/2009/05/tips-and-tricks-resources.html) and the Northwest Digital Archives (see http://orbiscascade.org/index/cms-filesystem-action/nwda/files/swg_cont_list_wf_20101210.pdf).

has developed an application, called Steady, specifically to convert data in spreadsheets to EAD.[22] Once data has been converted to XML, an XSLT stylesheet may be used to further manipulate the data.

Webforms. Some institutions have developed webforms that allow for the production of EAD data. The Online Archive of California (OAC) offers several examples of webforms used to produce EAD finding aids, including such tools as EAD Web Templates and RecordExpress.[23] Using RecordExpress, archivists are able to enter descriptive data and publish that data in the Online Archive of California using the same Web interface. RecordExpress also offers the ability to upload PDF inventories, which will be indexed and searchable in the OAC. This approach could be very valuable for smaller institutions unable to commit to encoding all of their descriptive data in EAD.

EADitor is a tool for the creation and editing of EAD finding aids built on Xforms. In addition to forms that serve as a data entry interface for EAD finding aids, EADitor can be integrated with existing content management systems in order to publish finding aids, but it "includes an easily customizable public interface for searching, sorting, and browsing collections of finding aids."[24]

Text and XML Editors. Repositories may also use commercially available XML or text editors to create and encode EAD finding aids. XML and text editors are most suited for collection-level description but can be inefficient when creating or encoding inventories or EAD components. Many text editors, such as oXygen and Notetab Pro, allow for the use of macros, scripts, or other tools that at least partially automate the process of encoding. Tools such as oXygen and XMetaL also offer multiple "views" of the EAD data, allowing staff to see the data as a text document with or without XML tags or even as data entry forms (see Figure 7). These features can often be customized; for example, oXygen relies on a CSS stylesheet, which controls display properties for its "author view."

Creating descriptive records in XML and text editors may not be the most efficient approach, particularly for repositories utilizing volunteers or undergraduate student employees for data entry projects.

---
22 For more information about Steady, see http://steady.heroku.com/pages/about.
23 More information is available through the Online Archive of California EAD toolkit, available at http://www.cdlib.org/services/dsc/tools/ead_toolkit.html.
24 For more information on EADitor, see http://code.google.com/p/eaditor/.

164 ARCHIVAL ARRANGEMENT AND DESCRIPTION

For most repositories, however, there are a number of benefits to developing at least some staff expertise in creating and manipulating XML documents. As the *Barriers to EAD* report states:

> In-house conversion [of finding aid data to EAD] offers numerous benefits: fostering staff skills, flexibility in schedule and workflow, and direct control over process and inputs. Basic XML skills are not difficult to acquire, and having internal staff with XML knowledge may benefit other library processes and projects as well. . . . Once you have gained confidence in understanding and defining the EAD output you expect, then any programmer with experience of scripting languages like Perl or VisualBasic and XML could write scripts to produce the desired output from your existing input.[25]

As with accessioning, many repositories will be tempted to create finding aids using word-processing software such as Microsoft Word. Archivists should avoid this strategy, if at all possible, unless the repository has a pre-established method for converting the word-processed documents to other, more structured formats. Creating descriptive data in a simple spreadsheet does not substantially increase the time it takes to perform data entry. It can, in fact, increase efficiency by allowing a processing archivist to analyze data using simple formulas to spot and correct errors or find bulk dates. Most importantly the structured data can be easily repurposed and converted to XML and other structured forms using the methods described in the accessioning section above.

Other Descriptive Data and Outputs

Many archival repositories have evolved beyond the point of simply creating traditional finding aids and publishing those finding aids on the Web. There are a number of other types of descriptive records and outputs that can be delivered as part of an archival access system.

Encoded Archival Context—Corporate Bodies, Persons, and Families (EAC-CPF). In 2010 the Society of American Archivists formally approved *Encoded Archival Content—Corporate Bodies, Persons, and Families* (EAC-CPF) as a standard for encoding contextual information about people, corporate bodies, and families that create archival material.[26] EAC-CPF allows archivists to describe the

---
25 Combs et al., *Over, Under, Around, and Through,* p. 20.
26 For more information about EAC-CPF, see http://eac.staatsbibliothek-berlin.de/.

Figure 7. Editing a Finding Aid Using oXygen XML Editor

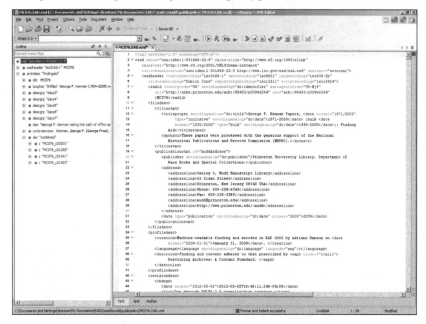

individuals, families, and corporate bodies that create, preserve, use, and are responsible for and/or associated with records in a variety of ways, as well as to establish their relationship to other records creators, to archival or other resources, and to functions or activities. EAC-CPF records contain three basic types of information:

- An identity section, which includes authorized and other forms of names that describe a particular agent (i.e., person, family, or corporate body);
- A description section, which includes biographical or historical information similar to that found in archival finding aids, as well as other descriptive elements such as dates of existence; and
- A relationships section, which demonstrates the person's, corporate body's, or family's relationship to other entities. The relationships section allows an archivist to include pointers and links to related resources (such as archival materials); to related persons, families, or organizations; and to functions or activities completed by the agent. Figure 8 shows a typical EAC-CPF record, drawn from the Social Networks and Archival Context Project website.

Figure 8. EAC-CPF Record

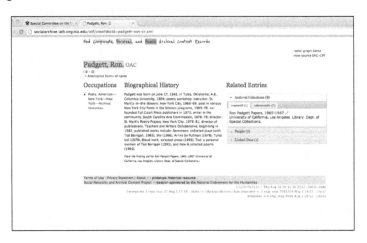

Because it is a new standard, fewer tools are available to automate the production of EAC-CPF records. ICA-AtoM and Archon currently support the export of authority records as EAC-CPF records, and ArchivesSpace will provide a similar feature. In many cases, however, the most efficient way to produce EAC-CPF is to extract data from EAD records through the use of XSLT or XQuery transformations. For example, data related to the creator of each archival collection in an EAD file (such as the <origination> and <bioghist> elements) can be used to create an EAC-CPF file. Repositories can use tools such as oXygen to perform these types of transformations. As the standard matures, more tools, procedures, and projects should develop to assist in the creation of EAC-CPF records. The most prominent U.S.-based project as of this writing is the Social Networks and Archival Context (SNAC) Project, which is funded by the Andrew W. Mellon Foundation. The project aims to create a set of tools and procedures that will facilitate the creation of EAC-CPF records as well as a prototype public resource that allows users to browse EAC-CPF records and the resources to which they are linked. EAC-CPF records can, of course, also be produced by hand coding XML.

Digital Object Metadata. Archival repositories are often involved in efforts related to digitization and digital libraries, which make use of different or related descriptive standards, such as those described by Sibyl Schaefer and Janet M. Bunde in Module 1, *Standards for Archival*

Description in Trends in Archives Practice. Repositories can use many of the tools and procedures referred to above to produce records in these formats, such as XML-based MODS or Dublin Core files. As discussed previously, adherence to DACS or another content standard can greatly facilitate mappings and conversions between standards. The Archivists' Toolkit includes a Digital Objects module that allows for the creation of MODS and Dublin Core records, partially repurposing data in the AT's Resources module, as well as the creation of METS records for structural metadata.

Managing Legacy Data

Most archival repositories have created descriptive data for years, sometimes decades, in a variety of forms. In implementing a descriptive and access system, appropriately managing such data is often as important as creating new descriptive information. In many cases, it may be the quickest way to exponentially increase access to archival materials. In recommending that archivists leverage the data they already have, the authors of the *Barriers to EAD* report argue, "[i]n an increasingly online world, making your collection descriptions as accessible as possible to the widest possible audience is of paramount importance. Access deferred is access denied."[27]

One basic step that many archival repositories can take to increase the discoverability of their collection descriptions is to convert MARC catalog records to EAD or even HTML or PDF and then to post the resulting records online. While MARC records remain a viable option for many smaller and academic repositories, most library public access systems require users to search specific databases on specific websites, unlike finding aids, which are more easily indexed by common Internet search engines.

Transformations from MARC to EAD can be accomplished in a number of ways. The most common tool for such transformations is MarcEdit, a free tool developed at Oregon State University (see Figure 9). MarcEdit, which relies primarily on XSLT transformations, provides an easy-to-use interface, which allows users to simply select a MARC record and convert it to another structured format such as EAD. Archivists may need to tweak the MARC-to-EAD stylesheet

---

27 Combs et al., *Over, Under, Around, and Through*, 12.

Figure 9. MarcEdit Conversion of MARC Record to EAD

that is provided with the software to match their own practices, but a number of repositories have already undertaken this work.[28]

When working with legacy data, archivists should strive to convert data into a format that meets modern archival descriptive standards. Structured data is the easiest to manage and to convert to current descriptive standards, particularly if the data is stored in a relational database or even spreadsheets. From these sources, it can be mapped to descriptive elements and output as EAD, MARC, or other structured records through automated methods. In addition to the built-in tools available within common database and spreadsheet applications, other free tools offer powerful options for manipulating and cleaning up data. For example, Google Refine is, according to its website, "a power tool for working with messy data."[29]

---

28 For example, the Seeley G. Mudd Manuscript Library and Department of Rare Books and Special Collections at Princeton University have developed XSLT stylesheets for this purpose. Also see MarcEdit, http://people.oregonstate.edu/~reeset/marcedit/html/index.php.

29 Google Refine home page, accessed October 13, 2012, http://code.google.com/p/google-refine/.

In the case of unstructured data, more work will be needed. Data in word-processed documents is typically less structured and more complicated to convert to EAD or other structured forms. Descriptive information in tables or separated by tabs can sometimes be converted to spreadsheets, but the data must have been entered consistently to easily automate conversion. In some cases, archivists can write scripts or macros to recognize patterns in word-processed documents and insert appropriate EAD tags around descriptive elements, such as titles and dates. NoteTab Pro, in particular, offers a clip library and macro language that allows users to automate many common tasks. A number of NoteTab Pro templates and tools related to EAD were developed in conjunction with the EAD Cookbook in the early 2000s and are still available for use.[30] Archivists familiar with regular expressions can use this powerful tool to find and manipulate patterns in strings of text. Regular expressions can be complex to understand and write, but those who master them gain a tremendous advantage in wrestling with messy descriptive data. They can be used in conjunction with a wide variety of software, including tools like Google Refine or XML editors such as oXygen.

Descriptive data that exists only in hard copy, such as typewritten finding aids and lists or card catalogs, is often the most difficult to convert to structured forms. Typewritten finding aids can sometimes be scanned, with the resulting images run through an Optical Character Recognition (OCR) process.[31] The files can then be treated in the same manner as word-processed files.

Smaller repositories with limited financial resources but with well-managed undergraduate student or volunteer programs may find that the most efficient method to convert hard-copy descriptive records to electronic form is rekeying. This approach, which requires careful planning, data mapping, and direction but little administrative overhead and training, can yield high data entry rates.

Repositories with appropriate financial resources may choose to outsource conversion of legacy finding aids and other data. Vendors

---

30 As of 2012, the EAD Cookbook was available through the EAD Roundtable of the Society of American Archivists, which maintains a GitHub site with tools related to EAD production and delivery. See http://saa-ead-roundtable.github.com/.
31 There is a wide variety of OCR software available, from free and open-source products to commercial tools such as BBYY FineReader. OCR functionality is also built into some general-purpose tools such as Adobe Acrobat.

often charge a per-page (for hard-copy documents) or per-byte (for electronic files) conversion rate. Outsourcing projects require considerable up-front work in communicating needs and expectations to vendors. As in all descriptive work, ensuring adherence to DACS is an important part of any project.

OCLC Research's report, *Over, Under, Around, and Through: Getting Around Barriers to EAD Implementation* by Michele Combs et al., (2010), contains a useful discussion of the issues regarding conversion of legacy data to EAD and includes a decision-making matrix that is useful for repositories undertaking a legacy data conversion project.[32]

Reducing Backlogs and Managing Collections

Data conversion projects are often a necessary part of designing an archival descriptive and access system, but what happens when a repository lacks any significant data for collections in its holdings? Archivists have been grappling with the problem of backlogs for years, but increased attention has been focused on the issue since the publication of Mark Greene and Dennis Meissner's 2005 article "More Product, Less Process" (known colloquially as MPLP).[33] Although all of the tools listed in the section regarding description are relevant to a backlog reduction project, a number of tools and strategies are specifically designed to help repositories gather basic information about their holdings and to repurpose that information as descriptive records.

The concept of the collection assessment has received significant attention over the last several years. Several repositories and consortia have undertaken efforts to systematically record and assess their holdings. Most of these efforts involve surveying the entirety of a repository's holdings and recording ratings data for each collection in categories such as level of description, level of arrangement, physical condition, and research value. Recording this type of data can be enormously useful for setting processing and digitization priorities, which are necessary steps involved with designing any archival access system. Many survey projects incorporate the creation of descriptive data, either during the survey or as a future step, and also typically

---

32 Combs et al., *Over, Under, Around, and Through*, 19–22.
33 Mark A. Greene and Dennis Meissner, "More Product, Less Process: Revamping Traditional Archival Processing," *American Archivist* 68 (Fall/Winter 2005): 208–263.

involve the verification of locations and holdings information, which are necessary parts of any access system that incorporates request and circulation functions.

Martha O'Hara Conway and Merrilee Proffitt's 2011 OCLC Research report *Taking Stock and Making Hay: Archival Collections Assessment* lists institutions that have undertaken collection survey and assessment projects.[34] To date, most institutions have designed purpose-built databases to support such projects. For example, the Philadelphia Area Consortium of Special Collections Libraries (PACSCL) surveyed and created assessment and descriptive data for more than 2,100 collections at 22 institutions in Philadelphia using a locally designed FileMaker Pro database (see Figure 10). The descriptive data fields in the database were mapped to DACS elements. The database supports exports for collection-level EAD records, as well as MARC XML. Other institutions have designed databases using Microsoft Access or other commercially available database software. Repositories with extremely limited information technology resources or technical expertise can create a simplified version of an assessment database by entering ratings information into a spreadsheet and by using an identifier for each collection, such as a collection or call number, to ensure that the ratings can be associated with appropriate collections.

The current version of the Archivists' Toolkit also includes an Assessment module, shown in Figure 11.[35] It supports data entry for collection ratings using the PACSCL project ratings categories, linking the assessment records to accession or resource records. Archivists can use the assessment data to produce reports and track levels of access. Because the assessment records are linked to descriptive records in the Archivists' Toolkit Resource module, they can easily be tracked and enhanced as needed.

Collection management databases are valuable resources in gaining intellectual control of archival holdings. Implementing these tools can be an important foundational step in designing and implementing a descriptive and access system, particularly in cases in which other descriptive information is lacking or an archives is just beginning to organize a large backlog with many descriptive and access needs.

---

34 Martha O'Hara Conway and Merrilee Proffitt, *Taking Stock and Making Hay: Archival Collections Assessment* (Dublin, OH: OCLC Research, 2011), accessed November 18, 2012, http://www.oclc.org/research/publications/library/2011/2011-07.pdf.

35 Note that there is some question about whether the Assessment module will be supported in the first development phase of ArchivesSpace.

Figure 10. PACSCL Consortial Survey Database, Data Entry Screen

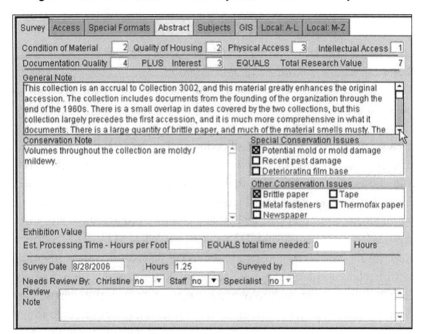

Delivering Descriptive Data and Providing Patron Access

The goal of any archival access system is to deliver descriptive data and archival content to users. In the twenty-first century, all cultural heritage institutions should strive to deliver their finding aids and other descriptive records online. Corporate archives that primarily meet needs within their own institutions may be prevented from providing broad online access to their holdings but will still likely be required to provide some level of networked access to employees. Meeting these goals can be challenging, particularly for smaller organizations, but a variety of methods and tools do exist. As with the creation of descriptive data, the methods and tools that each institution uses to deliver data to users will depend on the institution's goals and resources.

EAD Delivery Mechanisms

Delivery of finding aids is the most common method for archives seeking to provide access to their collections. Larger repositories,

Figure 11. Archivists' Toolkit Assessment Module

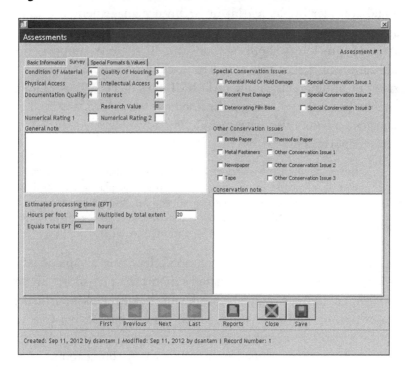

particularly academic repositories, often develop archival access systems built on EAD in its native XML format.

For repositories able to produce EAD files using the methods described above, the OCLC's *Barriers to EAD* report contains a thorough summary of publishing options for EAD:

> From simplest to hardest, these include: contributing records to a shared finding aids repository; delivering EAD directly to the browser; converting records to HTML or PDF for Web display; using inexpensive tools to enable searching of HTML and XML files; using an archival management system; and using an XML publishing platform.[36]

Institutions that have the option of contributing finding aids to a consortial or regional repository should take advantage of that option. Participation in a consortium frees repositories from the need to develop infrastructure for delivering EAD within their own institutions and benefits users who do not need to visit multiple websites to search for the information they are seeking.

---

36 Combs et al., *Over, Under, Around, and Through*, 23.

As in the creation of descriptive data, all archival repositories should consider implementing an archival management system that supports publication of finding aids and descriptive records. As discussed previously, both Archon and ICA-AtoM support direct publication of descriptive data. The Archivists' Toolkit supports the export of finding aids as raw EAD XML files or HTML or PDF files suitable for display through the methods described above. These management tools also have many other advantages. As the *Barriers to EAD* report states:

> By using archival management systems, archivists can streamline workflows, avoid duplicating data in multiple places, find and share information more easily, manage collections, and generate reports and statistics ... archival management systems can enable archives to create, manage, and share archival information more efficiently.[37]

Although archival management tools offer many advantages, there are some drawbacks. Installation and support of open-source archival management tools do require some technical skills. This is particularly true of Archon and ICA-AtoM, which require installation of a Web application and the access permission required to do so. Finally, while communities have developed around these open-source tools, support is informal and can be limited.

Commercial tools that support publication and offer the option of the vendor hosting data for the repository also exist, though these systems can be costly. Lisa Spiro's *Archival Management Software* (2009) offers a list of commercial products. Archival management software can also enforce relatively inflexible workflow and output, which can limit options for display and functionality, though this is typically only a concern for large and well-staffed repositories.

Archivists investigating collection management options should look for a system that includes the ability, at minimum, to import and export EAD files. In addition, the descriptive rules enforced within those systems should adhere to DACS or another archival content standard.

Delivering EAD directly in a browser is another relatively low-barrier approach to publishing EAD, though it does require some knowledge of XML and XSLT or CSS stylesheets. This option requires the insertion of a simple processing instruction into an EAD file,

---

37 Ibid., 24.

pointing to the stylesheet. When the processing instruction/stylesheet pointer is included in an XML document, XML files are transformed and styled like normal webpages in the user's Web browser. Most recent Web browsers support XML, but support for XML is not universal.

Instead of displaying the raw XML in a Web browser, it is also possible to convert EAD finding aids to other formats, such as HTML or PDF. As with the Web browser method, XSLT stylesheets are required to transform XML to other readable formats. Some software or command line scripts allow these transformations to run over multiple files simultaneously. Developing XSLT stylesheets requires some technical expertise, but several consortia and archives have made available XSLT stylesheets that archivists can adapt for their own institutions. The Society of American Archivists' EAD Roundtable maintains some XSLT stylesheets and related tools that repositories may be able to adapt for their own needs.[38]

Repositories can load HTML and PDF files that result from XSLT transformation to a Web server, where they can be viewed and indexed. Tools also exist that support indexing and searching EAD files without implementing a complex XML publishing infrastructure. The *Barriers to EAD* report describes several options:

> One example is Swish-e, "a fast, flexible, and free open source system for indexing collections of Web pages or other files." Google Site Search also provides an inexpensive, customizable way of searching Web pages.[39]

The most complicated—but often the most powerful—EAD publishing option is the use of an XML publishing platform. These systems allow XML data to be searched, browsed, and displayed. Implementing an XML publishing tool typically requires advanced technical skills, including both systems administration and programming ability. These tools are often highly customizable but require significant development time. Lists of XML publishing tools can be found in the *Barriers to EAD* report, as well as Lisa Spiro's *Archival Management Software* report. One tool that has gained traction among archival repositories and digital libraries programs is XTF, described on its website as "[a] flexible indexing and query

---

38 For more information, see the SAA EAD Roundtable at Github site: http://saa-ead-roundtable.github.com/.
39 Combs et al., *Over, Under, Around, and Through*, 24.

tool that supports searching across collections of heterogeneous data and presents results in a highly configurable manner."[40] XTF supports powerful searching, faceted browsing, and viewing search terms in context. XTF is an open-source product that is currently used by the California Digital Library in order to deliver EAD for the Online Archive of California. It is also used by Indiana University, the Social Networks and Archival Context (SNAC) project, and many other repositories or projects.

As mentioned above, some repositories lack the technical expertise or infrastructure to implement an archival management system or to produce EAD files. Options for delivery of finding aids that are not encoded in EAD are discussed below, although repositories should still concentrate on creating structured data that adheres to an archival content standard such as DACS.

Discovery Layers

Many academic institutions, both large and small, have begun to implement access systems that act as "discovery layers." These systems are designed to facilitate searching across multiple resources, such as library online catalogs, subscription databases, and local databases. These systems are usually seen as the entry or starting point for most library users. Archivists designing access systems should attempt to make use of these tools as much as possible.

The investment involved in ensuring that archival descriptive data is indexed and discoverable through these systems is likely to vary according to the tool and the goals of the repository. Many archival repositories will be content to simply index collection-level MARC records that include links to finding aids as an initial step. Though there is little user data available, it seems likely that indexing the entire content of finding aids in a discovery layer system would have a significant impact on access to archival material. Indexing the entire content of finding aids is likely to require significant planning and decision making, although, much will depend on the target system. Some open-source and XML-based systems, such as VUfind or Blacklight, may be able to index EAD files more easily than commercial products such as Ex Libris's Primo. Commercial products

---

40 XTF home page, accessed October 14, 2012, http://xtf.cdlib.org/getting-started-tutorials/fundamental-concepts/.

may require mapping EAD elements to a format understood by that tool, but the mapping should not be difficult if the user adheres to a content standard.

Non-EAD Finding Aid Delivery

Not all institutions will be able to create and deliver EAD files, or even to install an archival collection management system such as Archon, ICA-AtoM, or the Archivists' Toolkit. However, even institutions with fewer staffing and information technology resources may be able to download and install the Archivists' Toolkit on a local computer. Staff could then create descriptive data and output resource records as HTML or PDF files, which can simply be stored in a directory on a Web server. As long as these files are indexed by common Internet search engines, they should provide sufficient levels of access for most smaller repositories. Repositories whose resources are so limited that they cannot install a collection management tool such as Archivists' Toolkit or Archon may need to find creative options to deliver finding aids and other descriptive data online.

As discussed above, smaller institutions often have access to library systems and Online Public Access Catalogs (OPACS). Archival repositories unable to install a collection management system with a public access component should take advantage of library catalogs and OPACS if they are available. Repositories can deliver their collection-level records through the OPAC, placing links in records so that users can access HTML or PDF finding aids or inventories. If repositories create descriptive information in spreadsheets as described above, they can convert those spreadsheets to PDF and place them online in a directory.[41] Repositories with limited resources might even consider posting the spreadsheet files themselves, as they provide more advanced sorting and filtering functionality than most finding aid interfaces, though an access system that depends on multiple spreadsheet files may become difficult to manage over time.

Catablogs and Content Management Systems

As a last resort, smaller repositories should consider posting brief listings or collection descriptions to the website of their parent institution

---

41 Conversion to PDF can usually be accomplished through the spreadsheet software itself.

or to a free or inexpensive Web hosting option. For these repositories, one option is to create a "catablog" or to use widely available content management systems such as Wordpress or Drupal.[42]

A "catablog," as shown in Figure 12, is an archival catalog/website created with blogging software. It typically provides short descriptions of collections via blog posts. There are a number of benefits to catablogs. Because they are typically built using freely available and commonly used blogging software, they are usually easily implemented. Because collection descriptions are simply blog posts, they can be tagged and categorized, they can contain image and media files, and they can be easily shared through social networking applications. Perhaps most importantly, catablog entries can be easily updated and expanded when additional information or resources become available. If an institution is later able to implement a more traditional archival access system or to create fuller collection descriptions, they can simply be linked to the catablog entries or even exported in a structured format for relatively easy import to a collection management system or conversion to other structured formats such as EAD.

Although catablogs can be very flexible tools, the data delivered through catablogs should be made compliant with archival descriptive standards. As mentioned in the section about producing descriptive data, structured data mapped to an archival content standard such as DACS can be repurposed in multiple ways. Emma, the catablog maintained by the Brooklyn Historical Society, repurposes archival descriptive data through the use of a content management system.

Content management systems such as WordPress and Drupal are well suited for producing catablogs. These tools can also be used to manage content traditionally delivered on repository websites or "homepages," allowing for a more seamless experience for users. Once installed and configured, content management systems are typically easy to use; templates for blog posts or Web pages can be used to produce and deliver content, while themes can quickly alter and enhance the look and feel of the site. Communities have also developed around these tools, which has led to the development of plug-ins that provide additional features, like integration with social media tools

---

[42] For more information about the origination of the catablog, see Robert S. Cox, "Appropriate Technology and the Catablog," accessed October 13, 2012, http://www.pacsclsurvey.org/documents/cox/CoxProjDesc.pdf.

Figure 12. Catablog Example

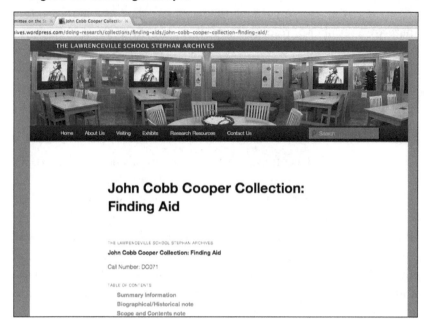

such as Twitter or Flickr. This integration provides repositories with new ways to publish information, allowing users to discuss content in familiar online environments such as social media sites.

In addition to content management systems, some archival repositories have used the open-source product Omeka. Omeka is "a free, flexible, and open source web-publishing platform for the display of library, museum, archives, and scholarly collections and exhibitions." According to its documentation and publicity, Omeka's "five-minute setup makes launching an online exhibition as easy as launching a blog."[43] Omeka also offers "Web 2.0 technologies and approaches to academic and cultural websites to foster user interaction and participation." Omeka has primarily been used to assist in the creation of online exhibits of archival material, but its website suggests other uses for archivists: "Use Omeka to share your collections, display documents and oral histories, or create digital archives with user-generated content."[44]

---

43 Omeka home page, accessed October 14, 2012, http://omeka.org.
44 "Omeka: Serious Web Publishing," accessed October 13, 2012, http://omeka.org/about/.

Relatively few peer-reviewed studies have been published concerning the use of content management tools for archives, but there are a number of resources available concerning the development of library websites using Drupal or WordPress. The *Practical E-Records* blog contains several posts concerning the installation and configuration of WordPress for the University of Illinois Archives website.[45]

Digital Objects/Digitization

In the twenty-first century, most users of archival material expect to view or acquire digital content directly through the Internet. All archival access systems should include a means to deliver archival material online, or, at minimum, to allow users to request digitization of material at a later date. Many archival collection management tools offer functionality that provides online delivery of digitized archival material. In addition, commercial digital asset management systems and tools developed with the Digital Library communities provide robust features for delivering and managing digital content.

Archon and ICA-AtoM provide features for delivering digital content to users. Many commercial products also are designed for this purpose, although fewer are designed specifically to fit the workflow for an archival repository. As with description and collection management functions, Lisa Spiro's *Archival Management Software* report provides a detailed comparison of various tools for this purpose. Common tools for delivering and managing digital content include commercial products, such as OCLC's CONTENTdm and Ex Libris's DigiTool, and open-source digital repositories, such as DSpace or Fedora.

In general, the open-source digital repository solutions are likely to require access to staff with significant technical skills and experience in installing and managing similar software. Commercial products may offer more technical support, particularly during implementation, but are often limited in terms of functionality and customization options. In addition, most repository and digital asset management systems presume that item-level control and description is desirable and achievable. Many digital library systems rely on the creation of structural metadata, in addition to descriptive records, when delivering access to digital content. This can often be a hardship

---

45 See Chris Prom's blog, *Practical E-Records,* at http://e-records.chrisprom.com/tag/wordpress/.

to even well-staffed archival repositories. Spiro sums up many of the options in her report:

> Many archival management systems offer a "digital library" or "online exhibit" function to provide Web-based access to items in their collections. In evaluating these features, archives should consider what kind of media and metadata formats they support as well as how media are presented. For instance, CollectiveAccess has rich features for media support, including the automatic generation of MP3s upon loading an audio file to the server, an image viewer with pan and zoom, and the ability to mark time codes within video files. However, some archives may want to use a dedicated digital asset management system (DAM), such as CONTENTdm, DSpace, or Fedora, to provide online access to their collections, since they are using these robust systems for other digital collections. These institutions will want an easy way to batch export relevant metadata from their archival management system or, even better, a way to plug in their archival management system to their DAM.[46]

Some archival repositories invest resources in implementing a "large-scale" digitization approach. Generally speaking, these efforts focus on increasing the amount of archival material that is digitized through reliance on traditional archival principles: selecting and digitizing material at the collection, series, or subseries level and relying on provenance and archival descriptive principles and standards in delivering these materials online. In most projects this involves linking or delivering digital images of pages through archival finding aids, instead of digital asset management systems designed to manage individual items, as shown in Figure 13.

Other options exist for smaller repositories. Many repositories utilize online photosharing sites such as Flickr to provide access to digitized images from their collection. These projects range from the large-scale efforts from the Library of Congress and Smithsonian through the Flickr Commons project to smaller-scale efforts from a wide variety of other institutions. Repositories using Flickr or a similar service in conjunction with their repository systems have reported a marked increase in the number of times images are used.

Instead of creating structural metadata such as METS files for digital objects, some repositories decide to scan the contents of entire folders of archival collections and bundle them as PDF files. PDF files

---

46 Spiro, *Archival Management Software*, 17.

are typically easy to create because most scanners and newer photocopiers can produce them. They also are a convenient delivery mechanism. Software for viewing PDF files is common and freely available and the format provides much of the same functionality that structural metadata does without the overhead of additional metadata creation. The PDF files themselves can be deposited in a repository or document management system, or even simply stored in a Web-accessible directory and linked from finding aids.[47]

Repositories can use many of the tools mentioned in this section to deliver born-digital content in addition to digitized material to users. Repository systems such as DSpace and Fedora, commercial products such as CONTENTdm, or, for the smallest repositories, basic Web directories or online document management services such as Google Docs or Dropbox can store and deliver digital objects linked from finding aids. The *Practical E-Records* blog provides an example of a workflow that results in the delivery of born-digital material to users.[48]

User Contributions: Patron-initiated Digitization, Description, and Crowdsourcing

Archivists have considered the possibility of user contributions to descriptive records for many years.[49] Interest in crowdsourcing and user-contributed description has increased in recent years in response to the growth of social media tools. In addition, as some archival repositories embrace MPLP-influenced descriptive practices that sometimes result in less-detailed descriptive records, enhancing description with user contributions can be an attractive option.

User-contributed description has several benefits. Researchers, whether they are experts in particular fields of study or genealogists, often possess more specialized knowledge than do processing archivists. They are also frequently able to spend more time with archival material, which can reveal insights that processing archivists may not discover. Finally, researchers often have relationships with others in

---

47 For a summary of this type of approach, see Daniel Santamaria, "Medium-Scale Digitization," presentation for the SAA Metadata and Digital Object Roundtable, August 2011, accessed October 14, 2012, http://www2.archivists.org/sites/all/files/mdor_presentation_2011_santamaria.pdf.
48 Chris Prom, "Simple E-Records Preservation and Access Plan," *Practical E-Records* (blog), 2011, accessed October 14, 2012, http://e-records.chrisprom.com/recommendations/supported-formats/simple-e-records-preservation-and-access-plan/.
49 Michelle Light and Tom Hyry, "Colophons and Annotations: New Directions for the Finding Aid," *American Archivist* 65 (Fall/Winter 2002): 216–230.

Figure 13. Delivery of Digital Images via an EAD Finding Aid

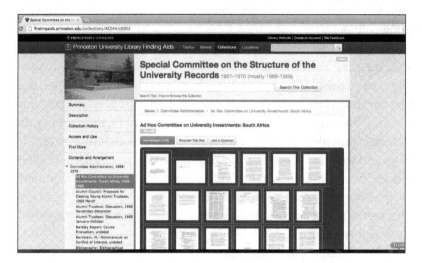

their professional communities and areas of interest. Providing a place for them to communicate, make connections, ask questions, and tell stories about archival material can have a powerful impact, not only in terms of enhancing descriptive records, but also in the promotion and use of descriptive records in general.

Few out-of-the-box solutions for crowdsourcing currently exist, but several high-profile projects have developed in recent years. The National Archives implemented a Citizen Archivist Dashboard,[50] which allows volunteers to transcribe,[51] tag, and create articles about digitized documents within the Archives' holdings. Transcribe Bentham is a participatory project based at University College London. Its aim is to engage the public in the online transcription of original and unstudied manuscript papers written by philosopher and reformer Jeremy Bentham.[52] The most high-profile project involving user-contributed data and archival finding aids was the Michigan Polar Bear Project. In 2005, a group led by Professor Elizabeth Yakel of the University of Michigan School of Information began a research project investigating next-generation finding aids. The group experimented with different

---

50 See the Citizen Archivist Dashboard at http://www.archives.gov/citizen-archivist/.
51 See the National Archives Transcription Pilot Project at http://transcribe.archives.gov/.
52 Tim Causer, Justin Tonra, and Valerie Wallace, "Transcription Maximized; Expense Minimized? Crowdsourcing and Editing the Collected Works of Jeremy Bentham," *Literary and Linguistic Computing*, May 14, 2012, accessed October 14, 2012, http://llc.oxfordjournals.org/content/early/2012/03/28/llc.fqs/04.short?rss=1.

ideas for displaying archival content as well as implementing added functions so that researchers could interact with online collections using collaborative tools.[53]

As part of an effort to redesign the way archival descriptive data and content is delivered to users on the Web, the Princeton University Library's Archival Description Working Group has experimented with user comments on finding aids in conjunction with development work on a new finding aids interface. As shown in Figure 14, the commenting feature is provided through IntenseDebate, a commenting system for blogs and websites. A product of Automattic Inc., IntenseDebate allows users to post comments on individual pages and to publish comments using other social networking services such as Twitter or Facebook. This software can be installed on any site through the use of a generic javascript snippet.[54]

Though large-scale transcription and crowdsourcing projects may be out of reach for many repositories, there are strategies that small and medium-sized repositories can employ that embrace the spirit of the larger projects. For example, Flickr and catablogs allow commenting, tagging, and social media sharing. Catablogs, in particular, are a low-cost, low-barrier option for soliciting user contributions and comments and gathering communities of users interested in the use of archival material.

As more systems and tools develop, however, archivists can make efforts to ensure that users are able to communicate effectively with repositories. Many of these efforts are related to the following section, "Evaluating Access Systems and User Services," and include evaluating the usability of finding aids and the use of archival terminology. An approach as simple as including a visible and obvious link or other means to contact a repository, send an e-mail, or share information about a collection or finding aid can be an important first step in establishing contact with users and can lead to significant user contributions, corrections, and enhancements to finding aids, though in a more manual form.

Archival repositories can also implement user-driven description and digitization programs even without soliciting and capturing

---

53 Magia Ghetu Krause and Elizabeth Yakel, "Interaction in Virtual Archives: The Polar Bear Expedition Digital Collections Next Generation Finding Aid," *American Archivist* 70 (Fall/Winter 2007): 282–314.
54 See the IntenseDebate home page at http://intensedebate.com/.

Figure 14. Commenting on Finding Aids through the Use of a Commenting System

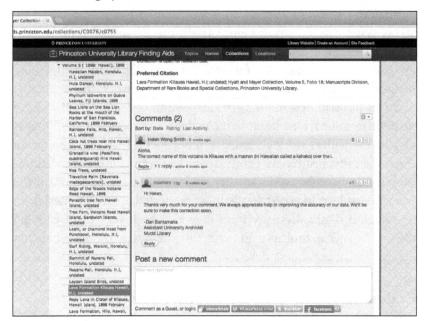

concrete descriptive data from users. Once a baseline level of description for all of a repository's holdings has been reached, the repository can record formal use statistics and analyze use patterns. Repositories can slate the most frequently requested collections for additional processing, description, and digitization. Analytics may also reveal that some collections are used infrequently and perhaps not at all. Processing infrequently used collections beyond a baseline level may not be an effective use of resources, but, through the availability of baseline-level finding aids, repositories can allow users to discover and request information about these collections. The repository may be able to provide additional description of these collections within an agreed-upon time period.

Similar methods can be used to create user-driven digitization programs. As discussed above, formal large-scale digitization programs seem out of reach for many repositories. Most repositories, however, will create copies or surrogates of material in their collection upon request. Several repositories have considered ways to capture the surrogates created using these methods. Perhaps the most robust patron-based digitization program was established at the Municipal Archives of Amsterdam, which allows users to request digital copies of material through finding aids available through the Archives' access system, as shown in Figure 15. In this case, the Archives links the digital files created for individual patrons to finding aids; the images are then available for future viewing by all patrons. Using these methods and an external vendor for the imaging work, the Municipal Archives has scanned millions of images and considers itself to have no digitization backlog because it can deliver requested digital images to patrons within weeks.[55] Smaller repositories may not be able to reach the same impressive productivity levels, but similar procedures should also be effective in smaller environments. In addition to the tremendous leap in access to the most requested archival material, an on-demand digitization program may also keep staff from copying the same material multiple times, freeing them to work on enhancing description of other, less-described material.

Evaluating Access Systems and User Services

Repositories should periodically evaluate the effectiveness of their descriptive and access systems. A number of methods are available for this purpose. When evaluating the success of an access system, it is important to use quantitative methods as a baseline measurement, though qualitative methods can also help improve services. Quantitative methods typically include data collection about the use of access systems and archival material. Some repositories also conduct usability testing and focus groups regarding their access systems.

A good first step for repositories deciding to conduct usability testing is to read through the literature regarding online finding aids. A number of studies conducted over the last decade address basic questions such as user reaction to archival terminology and traditional finding aid structure. Many of the questions asked and tasks performed by researchers can be adapted for new studies.

Repositories should also examine the "toolkits" created by the Archival Metrics project, which "seeks to promote a culture of

---

55 Ellen Fleurbaay and Mark Holtman, "You Ask, We Scan: The Amsterdam City Archives and the Archiefbank" (Plenary at the Mid-Atlantic Regional Archives Conference, Jersey City, New Jersey, October 30, 2009), https://webspace.princeton.edu/users/dsantam/archiefbank/You_Ask_We_Scan_%20Amsterdam_City_Archives_Low_res.ppt.

Figure 15. Municipal Archives of Amsterdam Digitization Request Interface

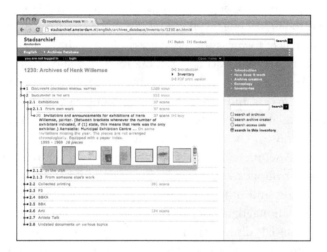

assessment in the archival domain by creating standardized user-based evaluation tools and other performance measures."[56] The project has produced a number of resources that archival repositories can use and customize when assessing their archival access systems. They include forms and methodologies for testing and recording data related to researchers, online finding aids, websites, student researchers, teaching support, and general website access tools, as well as a toolkit supporting focus group planning and implementation.

One of the simplest means to measure the effectiveness of an archival access system is to use Web analytics software. Basic analysis of server logs can reveal significant data about the use of archival access systems. This data can include the number of visits and number of unique visitors, visit duration and last visits, authenticated users, and last authenticated visits, days of week and rush hours, domains/countries of host's visitors, number of total pageviews, most viewed, entry and exit pages, operating systems and browsers used, referring pages, and phrases and keywords frequently used to find the site.

Many software packages capture data related to user behavior on and interactions with websites. The most advanced of these tools not only capture user data but present and format it in easily

---

56 For more information about Archival Metrics, see http://www.archivalmetrics.org/.

understandable ways such as through charts and graphs. There are many examples of free Web analytics software. Most of these tools, such as the popular Google Analytics, require a code snippet to be inserted into HTML pages but are relatively easy to implement.

Another way to measure the success of an archival access system is to track use of materials and remote reference and public services requests. Ideally, use and reference tracking systems should be integrated with archival access and collection management systems. Systems that integrate circulation, reference, and use tracking with archival access systems are limited. The most prominent commercial tool in this area is Atlas Systems' Aeon. Aeon allows users to register and request materials for viewing or duplication. It can be integrated into EAD finding aids, catalog records, and other databases. The data from these requests is stored in a relational database. Thus archivists are able to track requests for use of materials directly from the archival access system.

Additional options for tracking patron use include integration with a collection management system or design of a local relational database. The Rockefeller Archive Center has developed AT Reference, an extension of the source code of the Archivists' Toolkit, which provides functionality for patron registration, use tracking, and duplication of archival materials. In contrast to the approach of systems like Aeon, the AT Reference module requires staff to enter data for patron requests directly in the database. The AT Reference module has been released under an open-source license so repositories with sufficient resources can modify it to meet their own needs.

Perhaps the most common method of patron use and request tracking is the use of a locally designed database. Use-tracking databases can be designed with commonly available software such as Microsoft Access or FileMaker Pro and do not need to be particularly complex; at minimum, they should simply link patrons' names with the materials they requested.

Although not specifically related to use tracking and Web analytics, recording processing rates and other metrics related to description of archival material is an important aspect of evaluating a descriptive and access system. Collecting and recording data on processing rates and other archival functions can help repositories determine if the investment in their descriptive and access programs is returning meaningful results.

Joyce Chapman's "Return on Investment: Metadata, Metrics, and Management" is an excellent example of this type of work.[57]

Few tools exist for the comprehensive collection of data related to processing and description of archival material. In 2009 the Center for the History of Medicine at Harvard University developed a metrics database using Microsoft Access as part of the Center's CLIR-funded Foundations of Public Health Policy grant initiative, which was adopted or tested by a variety of institutions.[58] The database allows repositories to collect data on archival processing at a very detailed level. Institutions may be able to adapt the database to suit their own needs.

Because the collection of data about processing and description can itself be a substantial investment, data collection tools should be as simple as possible. Repositories unable to utilize tools like relational databases should consider recording basic processing rates in spreadsheets, which can be easily updated and shared between multiple staff people and provide advanced tools for data analysis.

Conclusion

The variety of systems and tools described in this module provide evidence of the complex and rapidly changing environment in which archivists find themselves. The tools are likely to change substantially in the next several years, particularly with the emergence of projects such as ArchivesSpace and with the integration of tools for managing born-digital archival material described in Module 2, *Processing Digital Records and Manuscripts*, in Trends in Archives Practice.

Though all archivists must make choices and analyze their resources and user communities when implementing descriptive and access systems, solutions do exist that will allow repositories to provide better access to the materials in their care. Archival repositories with very limited resources may rely on commonly available spreadsheet and database applications and content management systems. Many other institutions will choose to implement an archival collection management system. Some large institutions may develop innovative

---

57 Joyce Chapman, "Return on Investment: Metadata, Metrics, and Management" (paper, Society of American Archivists' Annual Meeting, August 27, 2011), accessed October 14, 2012, http://trln.academia.edu/JoyceChapman/Talks/65998/Return_on_Investment_Metadata_metrics_and_management.
58 "Processing Metrics Collaborative: Database Development Initiative," Harvard Medical School Wiki, last updated September 9, 2010, accessed October 14, 2012, https://wiki.med.harvard.edu/Countway/ArchivalCollaboratives/ProcessingMetricsDatabase.

local solutions. Regardless of the specific tools and systems used, archivists who create structured data and adhere to an archival content standard such as DACS will increase the possibilities for managing, repurposing, and providing access to the descriptive data they create. Doing so will help all archival repositories fulfill their ethical obligation to provide open and equitable access to the materials in their care.[59]

---

[59] Society of American Archivists, "SAA Core Values Statement and Code of Ethics," revised January 2012, accessed October 14, 2012, http://www2.archivists.org/statements/saa-core-values-statement-and-code-of-ethics#code_of_ethics.

Appendix A: Summary of Recommendations

Pre-custodial and Pre-accessioning Work
- **Simplest Option:** Create a simple spreadsheet or webform.
- **More Advanced Option**: Repurpose collection management software or locally developed database to collect data related to inactive records.
- **Most Advanced Option:** Implement a commercial enterprise records management (ERM) system.

Accessioning Archival Materials
- **Simplest Option:** Create a simple spreadsheet.
- **More Advanced Option**: Implement a locally designed database.
- **Most Advanced Option:** Implement an archival collection management tool, such as Archivists' Toolkit or Archon.[60]

Describing Archival Materials
- **Simplest Option:** Create structured data mapped to DACS elements in simple spreadsheets.
- **More Advanced Option**: Implement an archival collection management system and output descriptive records with no further editing and manipulation.
- **Most Advanced Option:** Implement an archival collection management system, supplemented with other specialized tools and post-processing routines, such as XML editors, XSLT stylesheets, and routines for encoding data from donors.

Reducing Backlogs and Managing Collections
- **Simplest Option:** Enter survey data into a spreadsheet.
- **More Advanced Option**: If already using the Archivists' Toolkit, implement the Assessment Module.
- **Most Advanced Option:** Design a relational database that maps to DACS elements.

Delivering Descriptive Data and Providing Patron Access
- **Simplest Option:** Post PDF or HTML finding aids in a Web directory. Link to digital objects when available. Alternate Method: Use a library catalog to deliver MARC records or create a catablog using a content management system.

---

[60] These solutions are not typically difficult to use or implement once installed, but they do require some degree of technical ability, access permissions, and infrastructure to set up.

- **More Advanced Option:** Implement Archon or ICA-AtoM. Alternate Method: Deliver styled XML output, or convert XML to HTML and post on a website.
- **Most Advanced Option:** Design a customized finding aid delivery platform with capability to deliver digital objects and capture user comments.

Evaluating Access Systems and User Services
- **Simplest Option:** Implement Web analytics software and/or create a simple local database to track onsite use and remote reference.
- **More Advanced Option:** Create a local use tracking database, in conjunction with periodic user testing using the Archival Metrics toolkit.
- **Most Advanced Option:** Implement an automated requesting system such as Aeon, in conjunction with website analytics and usability testing.

Appendix B: Case Studies

Princeton University Archives
by Daniel A. Santamaria

Seeley G. Mudd Manuscript Library at Princeton University is an example of a medium- to large-sized archival repository that uses a wide variety of tools in order to implement an archival access system. Though tools and procedures are evolving frequently, the access system has been quite successful, delivering descriptive data and digital objects to patrons despite some staffing and resource limitations.

Background

The Seeley G. Mudd Manuscript Library, a division of the Department of Rare Books and Special Collections of the Princeton University Library, houses the Princeton University Archives and a highly regarded collection of twentieth-century public policy papers. The more than 500 collections and 30,000 linear feet of archival and manuscript material in its possession are widely used by local, national, and international researchers. More than 2,000 visitors use the Mudd Library's reading room each year, and its staff field another 2,000 electronic, mail, and telephone inquiries annually.

In Fall 2007, staff at the Mudd Library reached a goal of providing online access to all of the Mudd Library's collections. This initiative involved a number of discrete projects, including several ambitious processing projects and a data conversion project resulting in the conversion of all legacy electronic finding aids to Encoded Archival Description.

Most significantly, basic descriptive data and location and holding information was created for all 335 collections, totaling more than 13,000 linear feet, held within the Princeton University Archives. This data allowed for the completion of collection-level MARC cataloging for all collections lacking descriptive records. The MARC records were then converted to EAD, primarily through the use of XSLT stylesheets and Terry Reese's MarcEdit software. Previously, more than two-thirds of the collections within the University Archives were not represented by any descriptive record online.

With the new EAD finding aids, descriptive records for all of Mudd's collections were discoverable in the Princeton University Library's OPAC, the Department of Rare Books and Special Collections' EAD website, union catalogs and databases such as OCLC's WorldCat and ArchiveGrid, and via common Internet search engines such as Google and Yahoo. As of June 2012, 504 records for Mudd Library collections were available.

Staff continue to add to the descriptive records through the creation of series-, box-, or file-level inventories, and as of spring 2012 all collections larger than 1 linear foot were represented with box- or folder-level inventories. The Mudd Library has also revised accessioning procedures to ensure that both collection-level MARC records and EAD finding aids are produced at the time of accessioning. Our commitment to descriptive standards and willingness to embrace new methodologies were essential in the success of the projects. We view these initiatives as quick, relatively low-cost and non-staff-intensive ways to enhance access to our collections. They have also led us to develop a view of description as an iterative process. We are able to expand or revise descriptions as collections are processed. We also view the descriptive records produced during this process as forming the initial descriptive infrastructure for digital library projects. We plan to use the EAD records to provide access to digital surrogates of material in our collections and to explore additional ways for users to interact with finding aids and the material that they represent.

The primary drawback of these methods is the large number of tools currently needed to accession, describe, and deliver descriptive records and digital content and to generally maintain our baseline levels of service. We continue to seek ways to refine our processes and our descriptive and access systems. In 2012, building on our previous work, we will redesign our EAD finding aid delivery platform, implement Ex Libris's Primo as a discovery layer for special collections material, and implement Atlas Systems' Aeon as a circulation and use tracking tool. These three tools will all leverage the structured descriptive data that we have previously created. We are also closely monitoring the development of ArchivesSpace in the hopes that it will help us further streamline and consolidate our descriptive processes and tools.

Description and Access Activities

Pre-custodial/Pre-accessioning

University departments and outside donors are required to complete a transfer form, which is a Microsoft Excel spreadsheet. In addition to contact information about the donors, we ask that at minimum a title, date, and box number are created for each folder to be transferred to the archives. We also ask donors to indicate if they are aware of any records that contain information that may be governed by federal privacy laws (typically, FERPA in the case of University records) or other sensitive information. The current version of the transfer form can be found online.[61]

Instructions for completing the forms and for contacting the archives are available on the Mudd Library website. We have also been experimenting with a webform created through Google Forms, which asks donors to provide additional contextual or domain-specific information about the material to be transferred. The current version of this form can also be found online.[62]

<u>Tools Used</u>: spreadsheets for descriptive data; Google Forms

Accessioning

Once the library formally takes custody of the material, whether it is analog or digital, an accession record is created in the Archivists' Toolkit. Basic descriptive and administrative data is entered for each accession according to documentation maintained at the library.

While electronic records and digital material are often transferred on physical media such as external hard drives or flash drives, the library has experimented with using document management and file sharing tools in order to transfer custody of records. The University's Webspace service, built on a document management system called Zythos, allows the library to set up a "dropbox" that university offices and departments can use to deposit electronic files.

Description is considered part of accessioning work at the Mudd Library. Each newly accessioned collection is described with a a DACS single-level optimum descriptive record in both MARC and EAD and published in the library's OPAC and finding aids website. Tools for

---
61 http://www.princeton.edu/~mudd/news/transf_donations/transf_instr/transmit.xls
62 https://docs.google.com/spreadsheet/viewform?hl=en_US&formkey=dENydVlHeG9nanJ6bWpHQ0JyR0MxZ3c6MQ#gid=0

describing newly accessioned collections and collections already at the library are the same and are described below.

Tools Used: Archivists' Toolkit Accessions module; Voyager Integrated Library System; spreadsheets containing descriptive data that are submitted by donors; Webspace/Zythos for electronic file transfer

Description

Creating New Data. Collection-level records are created in both MARC and EAD for all collections held at the library. Generally, collection-level MARC records are created and published in Voyager and then converted to EAD using MarcEdit. Inventories are created for any collection larger than 1 linear foot. These inventories are typically created using the Archivists' Toolkit Resource module unless data already exists in another structured form, such as a spreadsheet created by a donor.

Though this workflow uses a variety of tools, it is currently easier for us to initially create data using our library system and then transform it to EAD, rather than edit MARC-XML records produced by the Archivists' Toolkit. For small edits and additions to finding aids, it is also much more efficient to edit XML files than export resource records from the Archivists' Toolkit. We anticipate streamlining this workflow and moving entirely to the Archivists' Toolkit for description in the next year, primarily because we will index EAD data in Primo, the Ex Libris company's discovery layer product, which will make MARC records in the library OPAC redundant.

Legacy Data. As mentioned above, the library undertook an ambitious data conversion project in 2006 and 2007, resulting in the conversion of nearly 1,000 finding aids from Microsoft Word, WordPerfect, and HTML to EAD. The overhead on the project was substantial; it required writing an RFP and evaluating several proposals, hiring a project manager, and performing quality control on the vendor's work. Overall, however, the project resulted in more finding aids encoded in EAD than could have been achieved through in-house means alone.

The retro-conversion project included only finding aids that existed in electronic form. Mudd Library finding aids that existed only in paper form were encoded using other methods. First, any collections that lacked collection-level records received DACS's single-level optimum records, using the methods described under backlog reduction projects below.

The records were first created in the library's integrated library system and then exported and converted to EAD using MarcEdit. Collections that were described in paper and typescript inventories were rekeyed, with data entered directly into the Archivists' Toolkit. Though we initially believed this option would not be particularly efficient, we found that the inventories that had never been converted to electronic form were wildly inconsistent and not standards-compliant. Performing the data entry for these problematic descriptions in house allowed archivists to evaluate and restructure the information on an ongoing basis. Combined with the fast rates of data entry achieved by the undergraduate students doing the work, the rekeying was a useful option for us.

Tools Used: Archivists' Toolkit Resource module; Voyager Integrated Library System; oXygen XML Editor; MarcEdit; spreadsheets for inventory conversion for specific projects (often large or complex); Syncro SVN client

Backlog Reduction and Collection Management Projects. As mentioned above, as of 2005 two-thirds of the University Archives lacked an online descriptive record, and much location and holdings data was outdated. In late 2005, we formulated a new approach to processing and description. The stated goals were to create an online descriptive record for every collection held at the library and to regain basic intellectual control by updating holdings and location information.

A simple Microsoft Access database was in existence, though it had been nearly a decade since the last formal effort to update it. A data entry form was created and populated with data that already existed; records included title, dates of material, extent, and shelving location. Staff then conducted a shelf read of the entire University Archives, updating this very brief descriptive and holdings information. Once completed, reports and search forms were created that assisted in paging and locating material. Reports also assisted in the establishment of processing priorities.

After the initial survey, one staff member was tasked with creating MARC records for each University Archives collection. The staff member used the database as the foundation for these records but also examined the physical material. These records met DACS's single-level minimum requirements and were created using the library's Integrated Library Management System with a template established at the beginning of the project.

Once creation of the collection-level catalog records was complete (more than 250 records were created in approximately three months), the MARC records were converted to EAD with MarcEdit. The resulting EAD records were loaded into the library's EAD database and increased access to the University Archives collections dramatically. After the creation of the collection-level EAD records, focus shifted to the creation of inventories, which could then simply be attached to the collection-level records. As of 2012, every University Archives collection larger than 2 linear feet was described in a box- or folder-level inventory available through the Princeton finding aids website.

Tools Used: simple Microsoft Access database; Voyager Integrated Library System; MarcEdit

Delivery and Patron Access

Descriptive Data. Data describing material in the Princeton University Archives is delivered to users through both the library EAD finding aids website and through Voyager, the library's integrated library system.

The EAD delivery infrastructure is built on Exist, a native XML database that stores each EAD file and allows for transformation, via XSLT stylesheets, to HTML for viewing on the Web. Exist is compliant with the Xquery standard, which allows for fast and efficient querying of the XML data and a built-in indexing system. As with other XML publishing tools, the implementation of Exist requires either a high degree of technical expertise or significant support from a technology unit.

In the fall of 2011, the Princeton University Library began implementing a discovery layer system called Primo. Primo is a product of Ex Libris Ltd. and is designed to index and deliver descriptive data from a wide variety of sources. The Department of Rare Books and Special Collections EAD working group has been investigating ways to deliver EAD data to users through this system. As of Spring 2012, this work was still in an experimental phase, but we believe we have found an effective way to utilize this discovery layer as a part of our access system. Our approach is based on the concept of "component records" derived from each EAD component. Complex XSLT transformations are used to create component records that meet DACS's single-level minimum requirements and are enhanced with several additional descriptive elements. These records are validated against a locally developed DTD and finally mapped and transformed to an Ex Libris-specified XML format (PNX) that can be indexed and delivered by Primo.

We plan to fully index and deliver our EAD in Primo by the end of 2012. At that time, we hope to cease using the library's integrated library system as a delivery platform, which will eliminate the need to create MARC records and remove a significant step in our workflow.

The University Archives also maintains a number of legacy databases, describing special format material, such as audiovisual items, artifacts and memorabilia, and files documenting students, faculty, and staff. The data describing this material is stored in separate relational databases. While these databases do allow patrons to search the data, they are, in effect, data silos, and we plan to deliver the data in these databases using our other access systems (our finding aids website and Primo) in the next few years. We are also exploring creating EAC-CPF records for each of the people listed in the student, faculty, and staff databases. These records would also be delivered via Exist.

<u>Tools Used:</u> Exist; Voyager ILS; Primo

Digital Objects. Digital objects are delivered using a variety of methods. Several digitization projects have been conducted in conjunction with the Princeton University Library's Digital Initiatives staff. These projects typically involve the creation of item-level descriptive records in the form of MODS records that meet DACS's single-level minimum requirements, creation of structural metadata in the form of METS records, and delivery of images through the Princeton University Digital Library interface, which is also built on Exist. These projects have typically been labor-intensive and resulted in descriptive records that were not integrated with the rest of our descriptive data.

Since 2008, the Mudd Library has been experimenting with linking digital objects to finding aids. This model relies primarily on PDF files produced on library photocopiers. The resulting PDF files bundle together the content, usually typescript or handwritten pages, described by each EAD component.

In this model the material described by each EAD component is treated as a single digital object. The principle is that, when creating the description, the archivist already decided that the EAD component represented the fundamental atomic physical unit. We want to rely on decision making by the processing archivist. We create no structural metadata and no item-level descriptive metadata. Practically speaking, common PDF viewers do many of the same things as systems built to take advantage of structural metadata. Each PDF is named using the bar code that was assigned to the physical folder. The only metadata used is the data that was previously available in that EAD component, with the addition of a <unitid>, which is intended to tie the original physical material to the digital object. We use library circulation bar codes for this purpose. A <dao> element is also inserted with the link to the object.

PDF files created for these purposes can be delivered to users easily; at the Mudd Library they are currently managed in the University-supported document management system, Webspace, which is described above.

Tools Used: Exist (for finding aid and metadata delivery); Adobe Acrobat/Reader; Webspace/Zythos or simple Web directory

Crowdsourcing Possibilities. The primary method for gathering user comments and data from finding aids is through the use of a "contact" link present at all times from all finding aids. The library frequently receives corrections and clarifications from users through this method, though it is a very labor-intensive process, requiring users to send e-mail and staff to read the e-mail and act on it. The user commenting feature described in the main body of this module is intended as an improvement to this process.

The University Archives has also implemented a blog entitled "The Reel Mudd," which features digitized content from the Archives and invites users to comment on the posts and provide additional information.

Evaluating Access Systems and User Services

Use Tracking

Use of material is currently tracked with a variety of methods. In-house circulation statistics are kept in a locally designed Microsoft Access database, which allows for the entry of collection call numbers and box numbers. Public Services staff log the call numbers of collections used to answer remote inquiries and that data is also entered into a locally designed database. Similar information is also tracked for photoduplication and image scanning requests. This information is used in a variety of ways, including the establishment of processing and digitization priorities.

As of July 1, 2012, the library has begun testing Aeon, an automated circulation and user registration system. Aeon sends structured data from EAD finding aids to a relational database. It allows sophisticated user tracking and collection of data. The library is also considering implementing Aeon's photoduplication module, which will allow users to request digitization of material directly from finding aids.

Web Analytics

Data on finding aid usage is currently collected using a service called AW stats. At time of writing, the library planned to implement Google Analytics to collect data regarding online finding aid usage. This data will be used to supplement traditional circulation and use statistics and will aid in the implementation of a patron-driven digitization program. For example, the top ten most viewed EAD components will be digitized each month.

<u>Tools Used:</u> local circulation database; Aeon; Google Analytics

Shelby White and Leon Levy Archives Center, Institute for Advanced Study
by Christine Di Bella

Background

Formalized in 2009, the Shelby White and Leon Levy Archives Center serves as the repository for the historical records of the Institute for Advanced Study. The Institute is a private academic institution located in Princeton, New Jersey, that exists to encourage and support fundamental research in the sciences and humanities. Work at the Institute takes place in four schools: Historical Studies, Mathematics, Natural Sciences, and Social Science. The Institute's most famous affiliate, past or present, is Albert Einstein, but more than thirty Nobel Laureates and nearly three-quarters of those awarded the Fields Medal have been associated with the Institute. The Institute is and has always been independent from its much larger neighbor, Princeton University.

The Archives Center collection dates to the founding of the Institute in 1930 and includes official correspondence of the Director's Office, minutes of meetings of the faculty and the Board of Trustees, correspondence concerning past faculty and members, records of the Electronic Computer Project, and the papers of select faculty members. This portion of the collection totals approximately 850 linear feet; other materials include the Institute's photograph and oral history collections, as well as a number of art and artifacts.

The Archives Center is a unit within the Historical Studies-Social Science Library at the Institute. It has two full-time staff—a professional archivist and a paraprofessional archival assistant. A part-time consultant conducts oral history interviews throughout the year. The Archives is not permitted to host volunteers or interns but receives temporary paid assistance from college students in the summer through an institution-wide employment program.

Like most repositories, we face a number of challenges in managing the material in our care and making it available to researchers in a timely fashion. Our greatest access challenges, far from unique among institutional archives like ours, include the following:

- Although the presence of a full-time archivist at the Institute is a relatively recent phenomenon, use of our collections is not.

In addition to significant outside research, there is heavy use by internal constituents at the Institute, resulting in a substantial administrative reference load for the two staff members.
- As the only unit at the Institute responsible for preservation of its cultural heritage, we manage not just archival material but also nearly 1,000 works of art and artifacts.
- While the Institute itself has excellent IT support, there is none designated solely for the library and archives, and the Archives Center must vie for these limited resources with other units on campus with more pressing day-to-day requirements.

Our primary access objective in the Archives Center is to support our internal constituency to the greatest extent possible, but with an eye toward making our collections and resources discoverable by those outside the Institute with related professional or personal research interests.

Description and Access Activities

Pre-custodial/Pre-accessioning

The Archives Center acquires collections from Institute offices, from Institute affiliates such as faculty members, and from private donors outside the Institute. Instructions for transferring administrative records and general guidelines for private donations are available on the website for the Archives. Offices at the Institute are strongly encouraged to submit box lists created in Excel listing the contents of transfers. On the other hand, we get a wide variety of information relating to privately donated material, ranging from detailed contents lists to verbal descriptions of collections. In most cases, if no contents list is available from the donor, we create one in Archivists' Toolkit at the time of accessioning, using information available within the collection.

Tools Used: website, Microsoft Excel

Accessioning

Archivists' Toolkit (AT) is our primary collection management system for archival collections. (As the Institute had no formal accessioning program for archival collections before 2009 and all documentation was paper-based, our implementation of this system in 2009 was a major step forward in the professionalization of the Archives.) At the time of receipt, we create an accession record in AT. We create accession records for both analog and digital collections. For digital collections, we take the additional step of processing the files using Duke's Data Accessioner and storing the resulting files and metadata on our shared file server.

PastPerfect is our primary collection management system for art and artifacts. The license for this system was purchased before 2009, and as it has proven inexpensive to maintain and better suited than the AT for these types of materials, we have continued to use it. We acquire art and artifacts less frequently than archival material (most of our cataloging in PastPerfect has involved documenting acquisitions retrospectively), but when we do, we create a record in PastPerfect.

Tools Used: Archivists' Toolkit, Duke Data Accessioner, and PastPerfect. At this time, we are considering using Archivematica to accession digital records in place of the Data Accessioner, because future releases are expected to provide capability to integrate with our system for access, CONTENTdm.

Description

Creating New Data. We create new data for archival collections in AT. For art and artifacts, we create data in PastPerfect. Over the last two years, our summer student workers entered folder-level information in AT for nearly all collections that did not have it from another source, and a temporary employee cataloged most of our art and artifacts in PastPerfect. In addition to creating contents lists as needed, prospectively, when we receive a contents list from an Institute office or individual donor, we encode it in EAD and import it into AT for inclusion in the resource record.

At this time, we do not create MARC records for our collections. Because we take an iterative approach to description, we find it burdensome to make changes in multiple places given our staffing level.

Legacy Data. Though not formalized until 2009, the Institute has managed archival collections since the mid-1980s. While only one collection had a traditional finding aid before 2009, detailed folder-level MARC records had been created for some of the most heavily used collections and individual items (such as photographs); this work was completed years earlier in a staff-only database in the library's online catalogue, Horizon. With the help of the Institute's Historical Studies-Social Science librarian, who used BibBase (the predecessor system to Horizon at the Institute) to convert MARC records to files that could then be encoded in EAD, we were able to import information from the catalog records into AT records.[63] We also sometimes use the tab-delimited text output of MarcEdit for this purpose, because the software is free and well known to the staff in the Archives. The cataloging in Horizon is very detailed but inconsistent, often containing dozens of added name and subject headings. We decided not to carry these over to AT, but staff consult Horizon on occasion, to answer certain types of reference questions.

Tools Used: Archivists' Toolkit; Microsoft Excel for encoding contents lists received from offices; PastPerfect; MarcEdit; Horizon/BibBase

Delivery and Patron Access

Descriptive Data. To deliver descriptive information to our users, we use a slightly revised version of AT's HTML report for finding aids, which we paste into a Drupal-based institutional Web template. All finding aids are linked from the Archives website. The Institute website has a Google site search box, and the contents of the finding aids are discoverable via either that search box or search engines outside the Institute site. (There is no Archives-specific search engine for this material.)

Digital Objects. In 2001 we purchased a license for CONTENTdm to deliver our digital content. The system is locally hosted and maintained. In addition to the records for digitized images and documents created from scratch or adapted from AT or Horizon records, we imported data and images from PastPerfect to provide digital representations of our most noteworthy art and artifacts. We made the decision to buy an off-the-shelf product because our needs were sophisticated enough that we found we needed a content management system. We did not want to continue posting individual files on our website, but we knew

---

63 Generally we export titles and dates from the MARC 245 and 260 fields and convert them to EAD <unittitle> and <unitdate> elements. Other fields exist in the MARC records, but because they are inconsistently encoded, they would require significant manipulation and cleanup if they were to be converted to EAD, which is not possible for us at this time.

our limited claim to internal IT resources would make building our own system with an equivalent level of functionality challenging.

We provide links to digital objects in CONTENTdm from finding aids, and links to finding aids from CONTENTdm records. Because the online finding aids predate the CONTENTdm records in most cases, inserting these links in both places is a manual process. As we accumulate more and more digital content as a result of scanning projects and routine patron scanning and as our use of both AT and CONTENTdm matures, we are considering using the Digital Objects module in AT and delivering the finding aids themselves as EAD in CONTENTdm but have not yet made that move.

CONTENTdm provides options for enabling printing and downloading of images, documents, and other digital content. We have enabled printing for all records regardless of format, and we enabled downloading for documents. Though we currently fulfill most image and document requests via e-mail, by enabling the download functionality, we are able to use CONTENTdm to deliver large files (which exceed our e-mail system's attachment size limit) to patrons.

Crowdsourcing. CONTENTdm provides options for enabling rating, tagging, and commenting on images and other digital objects. We have enabled tagging and commenting on many records in CONTENTdm, though staff are currently the primary users of these features.

Tools Used: website; CONTENTdm

Evaluating Access Systems and User Services

To track reference requests, we designed a two-table Microsoft Access relational database and enter information about every request, including the amount of time to answer and the collections used. In this database we also track reference-associated scanning and photocopying.

Because active use of our access systems is relatively recent (less than three years old) at the time of this writing, we have not yet undertaken a formal usability review but will likely do so in the future as use of our system matures.

Tools Used: Microsoft Access

Appendix C: Selected Tools Supporting Description and Access

Tool	URL
Aeon	http://www.atlas-sys.com/aeon/
ArchivesSpace	http://www.archivesspace.org/
Archivists' Toolkit	http://www.archiviststoolkit.org/
Archon	http://www.archon.org/
Blacklight	http://projectblacklight.org/
Contentdm	http://www.contentdm.org/
DigiTool	http://www.exlibrisgroup.com/category/DigiToolOverview
Drupal	http://drupal.org/
DSpace	http://www.dspace.org/
EADitor	http://code.google.com/p/eaditor/
Ex Libris Primo	http://www.exlibrisgroup.com/category/PrimoOverview
Fedora	http://fedora-commons.org/
FileMaker Pro	http://www.filemaker.com/products/filemaker-pro/
Flickr	http://www.flickr.com/
Google Analytics	http://www.google.com/analytics/
Google Docs	https://docs.google.com/
Google Forms	http://www.google.com/google-d-s/forms/
Google Refine	http://code.google.com/p/google-refine/
ICA-AtoM	http://www.filemaker.com/products/filemaker-pro/
IntenseDebate	http://intensedebate.com/
MarcEdit	http://people.oregonstate.edu/~reeset/marcedit/html/index.php
Microsoft Access	http://office.microsoft.com/en-us/access/
Microsoft Excel	http://office.microsoft.com/en-us/excel/
NoteTab Pro	http://www.notetab.com/notetab-pro.php
Omeka	http://omeka.org/
Online Archive of California: EAD Toolkit	http://www.cdlib.org/services/dsc/tools/ead_toolkit.html
OpenOffice Base	http://www.openoffice.org/product/base.html
OpenOffice Calc	http://www.openoffice.org/product/calc.html
OpenOffice Writer	http://www.openoffice.org/product/writer.html
oXygen	http://www.oxygenxml.com/
Processing Metrics Database	https://wiki.med.harvard.edu/Countway/ArchivalCollaboratives/ProcessingMetricsDatabase
VUfind	http://vufind.org/
WordPress	http://wordpress.com/
XTF	http://xtf.cdlib.org/

Appendix D: Further Reading

A number of recent publications provide additional information that is directly related to efforts to design and implement archival access systems. As an excellent overview and articulation of a vision of modern archival descriptive and access systems, Max J. Evans's "Archives of the People, by the People, and for the People" (*American Archivist* 70 [Fall/Winter 2007]: 387–400), is an important and valuable contribution to the archival literature.

The major contribution to archival processing since the publication of Kathleen Roe's *Arranging and Describing Archives & Manuscripts* was Mark Greene and Dennis Meissner's "More Product, Less Process: Revamping Traditional Archival Processing" (*American Archivist* 68 [Fall/Winter 2005]: 208–263). Archivists and others interested in further reading about archival processing should consult both of these texts, as well as several responses to Greene and Meissner in the Spring/Summer 2010 issue of *American Archivist*. Greene and Meissner also summarized the reaction to MPLP in the *Journal of Archival Organization* in 2010 ("More Application with Less Appreciation: The Adopters and Antagonists of MPLP," *Journal of Archival Organization* 8, no. 3–4 [2010]: 174–226).

Archivists attempting to design and implement descriptive and access systems in the twenty-first century must address issues related to archival born-digital content. These topics are covered in Gordon Daines' Module 2, *Processing Digital Records and Manuscripts*, in Trends in Archives Practice.

As noted previously, Lisa Spiro's 2009 report on archival collection management software is a valuable resource for any repository investigating collection management tools. OCLC Research has published a number of recent studies covering related issues, including EAD implementation, large-scale digitization, and delivery of digital content—in particular, content generated in response to patron requests.

There is a sizeable body of literature concerning usability studies of archival finding aids. Archivists designing new access systems or simply evaluating their current systems should examine these studies. In addition, Chris Prom's 2011 *American Archivist* article, "Using Web Analytics to Improve Online Access to Archival Resources," provides guidance for using Web analytics software when evaluating the effectiveness of access systems.

There is a lack of published literature regarding the implementation and design of an archival access system that describes an entire archival workflow, from accessioning to delivery of descriptive records and/or surrogates and born-digital objects. Conference presentations help fill in some of these gaps in the literature. Following is a list of relevant conference presentations consulted during the writing of this module.

Articles and Publications

Bond, Trevor James, and Alan Cornish. "Developing and Sustaining the Northwest Digital Archives." *JODI: Journal of Digital Information* 9, no. 2 (June 2008).

Chapman, Joyce Celeste. "Observing Users: An Empirical Analysis of User Interaction with Online Finding Aids." *Journal of Archival Organization* 8, no. 1 (2010): 4–30.

Combs, Michele, Mark A. Matienzo, Merrilee Proffitt, and Lisa Spiro. *Over, Under, Around, and Through: Getting Around Barriers to EAD Implementation.* Dublin, OH: OCLC Research, 2010. http://www.oclc.org/research/publications/library/2010/2010-04.pdf.

Conway, Martha O'Hara, and Merrilee Proffitt. *Taking Stock and Making Hay: Archival Collections Assessment.* Dublin, OH: OCLC Research, 2011. http://www.oclc.org/research/publications/library/2011/2011-07.pdf.

Cornish, Alan. "Using a Native XML Database for Encoded Archival Description Search and Retrieval." 2004. http://hdl.handle.net/2376/1076.

———. "Utilizing Native XML: The Northwest Digital Archives Project." Presentation at the Washington State University Academic Showcase, Pullman, WA, April 1, 2005.

Evans, Max J. "Archives of the People, by the People, for the People." *American Archivist* 70 (Fall/Winter 2007): 387–400.

Exline, Eleta. "Working Together: A Literature Review of Campus Information Technology Partnerships." *Journal of Archival Organization* 7, no. 1–2 (2009): 16–23.

Gruber, Ethan, Chris Fitzpatrick, Bill Parod, and Scott Prater. "XForms for Libraries, An Introduction," *Code4Lib Journal* 11 (September 21, 2010). http://journal.code4lib.org/articles/3916.

Krause, Magia Ghetu, and Elizabeth Yakel. "Interaction in Virtual Archives: The Polar Bear Expedition Digital Collections Next Generation Finding Aid." *American Archivist* 70 (Fall/Winter 2007): 282–314.

Maier, Shannon Bowen. "MPLP and the Catalog Record as a Finding Aid." *Journal of Archival Organization* 9, no. 1 (2011): 32–44.

Patty, William Jordan. "Metadata, Technology, and Processing a Backlog in a University Special Collections." *Journal of Archival Organization* 6, no. 1–2 (August 2008): 102–120.

Prom, Christopher J. "Using Web Analytics to Improve Online Access to Archival Resources." *American Archivist* 71 (Spring/Summer 2011): 158–184.

Prom, Christopher J., Christopher A. Rishel, Scott W. Schwartz, and Kyle J. Fox. "A Unified Platform for Archival Description and Access." *Proceedings of the ACM/IEEE Joint Conference on Digital Libraries, Vancouver, British Columbia, June 18–23, 2007.*

Riley, Jenn, and Kelcy Shepherd. "A Brave New World: Archivists and Shareable Descriptive Metadata." *American Archivist* 72 (Spring/Summer 2009): 91–112.

Spiro, Lisa. *Archival Management Software: A Report for the Council on Library and Information Resources.* Washington, DC: Council on Library and Information Resources, January 2009. http://www.clir.org/pubs/reports/spiro/.

Walters, Cheryl D., and Sandra McIntyre. "Sharing Your Finding Aids in CONTENTdm: Encoded Archival Description (EAD) Files in Mountain West Digital Library." *Western*

CONTENTdm Users Group Conference. Reno, NV, June 2009. http://works.bepress.com/cheryl_walters/7.

Westbrook, Bradley, Lee Mandell, Kelcy Shepherd, Brian Stevens, and Jason Varghese. "The Archivists' Toolkit: Another Step Toward Streamlined Archival Processing." *Journal of Archival Organization* 4, no. 1–2 (2007): 229–253.

Yakel, Elizabeth, Seth Shaw, and Polly Reynolds. "Creating the Next Generation of Archival Finding Aids." *D-Lib Magazine* 13, no. 5/6 (May/June 2007). http://www.dlib.org/dlib/may07/yakel/05yakel.html.

Yako, Sonia. "It's Complicated: Barriers to EAD Implementation." *American Archivist* 70 (Fall/Winter 2008): 456–475.

Zhang, Junte, Khairun Nisa Fachry, and Jaap Kamps. "Effective Access to Digital Assets: An XML-based EAD Search System." *Proceedings of DigCCurr2009: Digital Curation: Practice, Promise and Prospects.* Chapel Hill, NC: University of North Carolina at Chapel Hill, School of Information and Library Science, 2009.

Presentations

Cox, Robert S. "Appropriate Technology and the Catablog." Paper presented at the PACSCL event, "Something New for Something Old: Innovative Approaches to Managing Archives and Special Collections," Philadelphia, December 4–5, 2008. http://www.pacsclsurvey.org/documents/cox/CoxProjDesc.pdf.

Di Bella, Christine. "Twenty-two Heads Are Better Than One: A Multi-Institution Approach to Addressing Backlogs." Paper presented at the PACSCL event, "Something New for Something Old: Innovative Approaches to Managing Archives and Special Collections," Philadelphia, December 4–5, 2008. http://www.pacsclsurvey.org/documents/dibella/01dibella.ppt.

Fleurbaay, Elleen, and Marc Holtman. "You Ask, We Scan: The Amsterdam City Archives and the Archiefbank." Plenary at the Mid-Atlantic Regional Archives Conference, Jersey City, New Jersey, October 30, 2009. https://webspace.princeton.edu/users/dsantam/archiefbank/You_Ask_We_Scan_%20Amsterdam_City_Archives_Low_res.ppt.

Ranger, Joshua. "Mass Digitization of Archival Manuscripts." Paper presented at the PACSCL event, "Something New for Something Old: Innovative Approaches to Managing Archives and Special Collections," Philadelphia, December 4–5, 2008. http://www.pacsclsurvey.org/documents/ranger/04ranger.ppt.

Santamaria, Daniel A. "Something for Everything: Thoughts on Archival Description at Princeton." Paper presented at the PACSCL event, "Something New for Something Old: Innovative Approaches to Managing Archives and Special Collections," Philadelphia, December 4–5, 2008. http://www.pacsclsurvey.org/documents/santamaria/02santamaria.ppt.

———. "Medium-Scale Digitization." Presentation at the Society of American Archivists' Metadata and Digital Objects Roundtable, August 2011. http://www2.archivists.org/groups/metadata-and-digital-object-roundtable/2011-annual-meeting-agenda.

Steman, Tom, Ian C. Stade, and Alexis Braun Marks. "How to Decide, Archon or Archivists' Toolkit: Open Source Software Solutions to Manage and Provide Access to Archival Information." Paper presented at the Library Technology Conference, St. Paul, MN, March 17–18, 2010. http://digitalcommons.macalester.edu/libtech_conf/2010/concurrent_a/25/.

Web Resources

Prom, Chris. *Practical E-Records* (blog). http://e-records.chrisprom.com/.

Society of American Archivists, EAD Roundtable website. http://www2.archivists.org/groups/encoded-archival-description-ead-roundtable/resources-maintained-by-eadrt.

University of North Carolina—Southern Historical Collections. Extending the Reach of Southern Sources: Proceeding to Large-Scale Digitization of Manuscript Collections. http://www.libunc.edu/mss/archivalmassdigitization/.

Appendix E: Sample Workflow and Tools for Small Repositories

This section provides recommendations and sample descriptive and access systems for small repositories that may have limited resources. Larger repositories will often be able to build on the basic concepts described below but may also be able to take advantage of many more of the tools listed in this module.

Small Repository Example 1:

Repository Able to Implement an Archival Content Management System

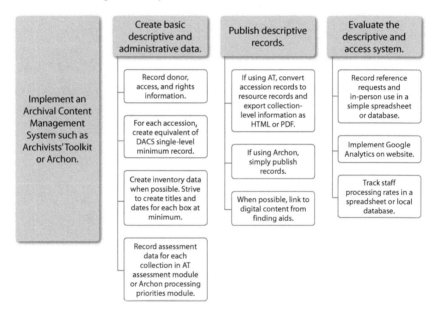

Small Repository Example 2:
Repository Unable to Implement a Content Management System

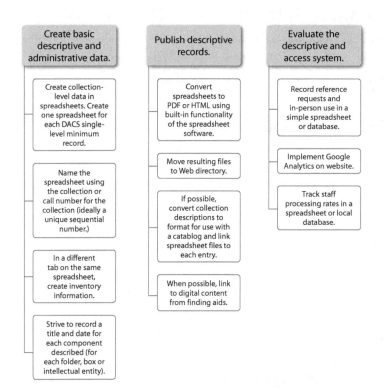

TRENDS IN ARCHIVES PRACTICE

ARCHIVAL ARRANGEMENT AND DESCRIPTION
Module 1: *Standards for Archival Description*
Module 2: *Processing Digital Records and Manuscripts*
Module 3: *Designing Descriptive and Access Systems*

RIGHTS IN THE DIGITAL ERA
Module 4: *Understanding Copyright Law*
Module 5: *Balancing Privacy and Restrictions: Personal and Family Papers*
Module 6: *Balancing Privacy and Restrictions: Organizational, Business, and Government Records*
Module 7: *Managing Rights and Permissions*

BECOMING A TRUSTED DIGITAL REPOSITORY (*Module 8*)

TEACHING WITH PRIMARY SOURCES
Module 9: *Contextualizing Archival Literacy*
Module 10: *Teaching with Archives: A Guide for Archivists, Librarians, and Educators*
Module 11: *Connecting Students and Primary Sources: Cases and Examples*

DIGITAL PRESERVATION ESSENTIALS
Module 12: *Preserving Digital Objects*
Module 13: *Digital Preservation Storage*

APPRAISAL AND ACQUISITION STRATEGIES
Module 14: *Appraising Digital Records*
Module 15: *Collecting Digital Manuscripts and Archives*
Module 16: *Accessioning Digital Archives*

. . . more modules to come!